Flight to Freedom

Rothenstem drawing of Squadron Leader Mike Donnet, 1943

Flight to Freedom

MIKE DONNET, D.F.C.

LONDON

IAN ALLAN LTD

First published in English by Ian Allan Ltd, 1974

ISBN 0 7110 0567 2

Published by Ian Allan Ltd, Shepperton, Surrey,
and printed in the United Kingdom by
A. Wheaton & Co., Exeter

Contents

Foreword

Lieutenant-General Donnet, writing in this book about his flight to England from occupied Belgium in 1941, says that "never despair and never give up hope" is an old adage. So it may be—but the words can rarely have been used by anyone who knows less about despair and whose hopes, against great odds in desperate times, never ceased to shine.

From our first meeting at Duxford in 1942, through renewed acquaintance some year or two after the War when I was serving for a short time in the British Embassy in Brussels, and during service together in Germany in the Second Allied Tactical Air Force from 1961–1963 where Donnet was my Chief of Staff, I have never known him to despair and I have never seen his hopes falter. I greatly admire his tenacity, his dash and determination, the ingenuity and imagination which he brings to every task to which he sets his hand. Tasks which have ranged from war-time escapes from Belgium in a light aircraft and subsequently fighting in the air with verve and courage over a very long period—unpretentiously recounted in this book—to participating in the peacetime command of large Allied air forces.

General Donnet's book, apart from being an evocative record of gallant flying, is a notable work on the history of the Belgian air contribution to victory in World War II. It stands as a tribute and memorial to those Belgians who died fighting for freedom and justice; it is an adventure story. Above all it will I am sure inspire those today, young and old, who cherish such ideals and hopes as those of Michael Donnet—a courageous and modest man who never despaired.

J.G.

Gibraltar
1974

Preface

Today is the tenth of May. The sun shines in a sky unspotted by a single cloud, and a light breeze stirs the apple blossom and the tender green leaves of poplar and lime. The warm air is full of birdsongs and last night the mellow-voiced nightingales sang to the stars.

Thirty-four years ago last night the nightingales sang in the woods of Notre-Dame de Bonne Odeur, on the outskirts of Brussels. But at sunrise came a roar of diving aircraft and the crash of bombs. Away on the eastern frontier the din of invading armour brought terror to a dumbfounded population, and on the Belgian pavé the rhythmic thud of the jack-boot resounded once again.

Without a single word of warning the Nazis had violated their solemn promise to respect Belgium's neutrality. Her allies' armies which, in the vain hope of remaining neutral, she had kept at arm's length beyond her western frontier, now moved up in a desperate but forlorn bid to stave off the invader. Once again Belgian and British dead lay side by side on Belgian soil, but the valiant resistance of the allied armies and air forces was of no avail against such a formidable array. Within a few days the country lay under the heel of a pitiless foe.

In the humiliation of defeat, the first thought of those who refused to believe in surrender was to escape and continue the fight on other fronts. One of these was the author of this book, then a young airman in his early twenties. Mike Donnet and I came of the same generation and we each had chosen the same métier. I say chosen, for there is no law in peace or war which can compel a man to adopt this métier; only volunteers are accepted as pilots or aircrew. We were pilots because some burning spirit in our young hearts could only be quenched by leaving the earth and soaring up to the stars. We flew for the love of it and the worst disaster that could befall us was, for some reason or other, to be 'grounded'.

In those early summer days of 1940 the personal situation of Mike and his comrades of the Force Aérienne Belge differed dramatically from ours in the Royal Air Force. Their country had been overrun in a lightning conquest; ours, with its ancient rampart, the sea, remained and continues to remain unmolested by hostile land armies. We were still free; Donnet and his countrymen were prisoners.

The sombre, tragic days unfolded Dunkirk, the capitulation of France and the final withdrawal into the island fortress which was England, there to make the last stand. The next few months were to see a critical victory won in the English skies and the invader, for the first time, thrown back.

Meanwhile Mike and his comrades, in duty bound, had allowed themselves to be led away into captivity, with all that it meant; forced marches, grim days and nights jammed together in cattle trucks, hunger and despair and . . . hope, the hope of one day reaching England, the last bastion of liberty.

How many times in the tormented history of mankind have force and evil seemed to be the deciding factors in man's destiny. But tyrants and conquerors do not reckon with the eternal spark of freedom which dwells in every human heart, and which tyranny and oppression do more than anything to kindle from a flicker into white-hot flame.

Donnet's only thought in defeat and captivity was to escape in order to continue the struggle, certain, like so many brave men and women in the conquered countries, that they would one day win back their lost liberty.

And so the amazing tale of his escape begins to unfold. Of the scant possibilities open to them, Mike Donnet and his companion Léon Divoy decide that the one which offers the best chance is to steal a tiny aeroplane, totally unfit to fly until long and patient attention under the nose of the enemy has put it back in working order. So, in the woods of Notre Dame de Bonne Odeur the conspirators, aided by faithful friends, including the valiant young Marc, Mike's 17 year old brother, go about their perilous and exacting task.

During the years that I lived in Brussels, I came to know and love those woods. This, and much more, the family ties that I have with Belgium, makes the story of Donnet and Divoy all the more poignant for me. The story has other aspects, too, which make it shine in the annals of man's eternal fight for liberty. Unlike myself and my comrades who were fighting, so to speak, on our own doorstep, the heroic resisters who came to join us from the enslaved countries had to leave hearth and home and abandon their loved ones to they knew not what fate.

Only the hope, alas not always realized, that they would one day be reunited, sustained their faith in victory. And so the years slipped by for them with little or no news from home, yet home was, by air, so tantalisingly close.

But perhaps the most touching thing for me in this story is the faith that the Donnets and the Divoys of those days had in England; that they should have slipped the chains that held them captive and come back, through endless perils, to join us as we grappled alone with the tyrant.

The critical Battle of Britain, with the fearful destruction by fire and high explosive that it brought to our cities, was already won by the time that Donnet and Divoy arrived. It was their turn now to help carry the fight back into the enemy's camp and this they did with unfailing courage, ever loyal to the cause they had joined, until victory brought them their greatest reward—reunion with their motherland and their loved ones.

This great story bears heroic witness to the faith of the thousands of men and women, who, in those grim days when all seemed lost, still had it in them to resist in the name of Liberty. May humanity for ever remember them.

La Mare aux Oiseaux,
St. Leger-en-Yvelines,
France
May 1974   Peter Townsend

I

Darkening Skies

August 1939 at a Belgian coastal resort. Sun-warm beaches, sparkling sea and a crowd of young and happy holiday friends.

For a young man in love with life and flying there were lots of laughs and high spirits. Alright, we said to each other. Even if Hitler *was* making threatening noises it was all bluff and the crisis would pass like it had the previous year. He knew just how far he could go. What was there to worry about in the future when for the present there were pretty girls to be flirted with and the prospect of flying again when leave expired in a few days?

At the end of the month these cheerful thoughts received a rude shock when the news broke that Germany had signed a non-aggression pact with Stalin. This jolted us somewhat out of our complacency but not until that fateful 3rd September when the panzers crossed the Polish frontier did it really come home to us that the hammer blow had fallen and that Europe was at war once again.

With other pilots of 9 Squadron of the Belgian Air Force, I listened in silence to our King's broadcast speech telling us that Belgium was to remain neutral. Privately we wondered how this could remain? How could we stay out of a general conflict which now seemed inevitable?

Our Squadron was based at Bierset, near Liège. We were a reconnaissance unit equipped at that time with the Belgian-built Renard machine. This was a high wing monoplane powered by a Rolls-Royce Kestrel 560 h.p. engine. We were one of sixteen squadrons which made up the Belgian Air Force in 1939.

Neutral we might be but that did not mean we had to remain unprepared. During the next seven months, the period of the "phoney war", more than fifty additional deployment airfields were prepared. At that time we used grass, not concrete runways, and any suitably level and large enough field could quickly be adapted for this purpose. The Army were mobilised and deployed along Belgium's natural first line of defence, the River Maas and the Albert Canal. We anticipated that if Belgium were invaded, British and French troops would move up to our assistance and our staffs got busy with plans for their deployment as well.

On our airfield, aircraft were dispersed around the perimeter and personnel moved out to requisitioned billets in the vicinity. The station hotel in Bierset became our Mess. A deployment airstrip was prepared at a spot half-way between Brussels and Liège. It was in the grounds of the Chateau of Durras near St. Trond and we noticed with appreciation how the thick woods, coming right down to the edge of this emergency airfield, would provide excellent camouflage for aircraft and vehicles.

As anyone who was with the British Expeditionary Force in 1939–1940 will remember only too well, that winter was wet, cold, and thoroughly miserable. Once, in November, we had a sudden general alert but it turned out to be a false alarm. I was lucky at Christmas and managed to get home to Brussels for a family reunion with my parents, my four brothers and two of my sisters. We thought it strange that my eldest sister, although living just a few hours away by car in France could not get a permit to cross the frontier owing to the emergency restrictions.

This period of uncertainty . . . of being on a war footing but not at war . . . was unsettling and depressing. Some of the younger pilots talked excitedly of the prospect of seeing action. In their minds they equated it with the job they had been trained to do. The larger issues; the pain, the sadness and the misery did not occur to them until much later when they saw their country engulfed, and overwhelmed in days; and felt the invader's boot firmly on them.

In mid-January it began to snow and the temperature dropped to a bitterly cold level. Again we had an alert, and in one night the entire squadron packed up and moved to St. Trond. We all thought it was just another false alarm. It was, in a way, but there was a difference. Much later I heard the true story. Apparently a German communications aircraft wandered off-course during a cross-country flight, carrying a staff officer. It made a forced landing near Liège and the staff officer was found to be carrying a complete invasion plan which envisaged a mass thrust through Belgium to the coast and was timed for that week. This, in fact was almost exactly what happened four months later but in this case the plan seemed to have been presented to us so fortuitously that the authorities decided it must have been a deliberate 'plant'. No one could accept that such a top-secret piece of intelligence could fall into our hands so easily!

The main thing I recall about this early alert was the intense cold in the unheated rooms of the Chateau annexe; many of them with broken windows letting in icy, stabbing draughts. Even with seven blankets over me in bed I shivered the night through without sleep.

We returned to Bierset with sighs of relief. At least our station hotel Mess was warm. Routine flying began again, mainly reconnaissance missions over the Albert Canal in the Leopoldsburg sector where the Cavalry Corps with which we co-operated were positioned.

At that time I was a pilot officer cadet. I had learned to be a pilot but now I had to learn to be an officer and a posting to the Officer School at Evere came through for me. Evere was quite a reunion since many of us had been together on initial training. There was Reuter, Genot, d'Hoogverst, Kirkpatrick and above all Divoy, with whom I was later to share the greatest adventure of my life. For the rest, many of them would not see another year, but we were not to know that then. At least there was still plenty of flying. The Observer School was at the same base so, after mornings spent in the classroom on military matters, we pilots were allocated to the task of flying observers under training in the afternoons. Not that we minded this additional job. My home at Stockel, a suburb of Brussels, was not far away and I managed several evenings at home.

In the middle of April the whole of the Officers School left Evere for the Armament Practice Camp on the coast at Ostende. We were to fly for air-to-air and air-to-ground gunnery training along the sand dunes and above the North Sea. On the 9th May, although leave had been cancelled the previous week, it had been restored and we looked forward to the Whitsun break in Ostende. The next morning the blow fell!

3

2

Invasion–1940

My war began at precisely 2.30am in the early morning of the 10th May, 1940. It was heralded by the loud voice of the orderly officer running through our quarters, switching on the lights and rousing everyone.

"Come on!" he yelled at me, throwing back the blankets. "Get moving! There's a war on!"

Bleary-eyed from sleep and still hardly knowing what was happening we tumbled out to the trucks waiting in the yard, engines running and drivers impatient to be off. We piled in and the cold air of the dawn just breaking through brought us thoroughly awake. Although we had half-expected it for so long, we heard with a feeling of incredulity that the Germans had begun their invasion of France and the Low Countries.

On the airfield a great deal was happening. All our fifteen aircraft had been pushed out of their hangars. They were trainers, a mixture of Potez, Avro 626 and Sv5 types. Their sole armament was two machine guns, one in front and one at the rear. The front one was not even synchronised. Not much with which to tackle the Luftwaffe!

Since I was one of the first into the back of the lorry everyone else had crowded in behind me and so I was last out. By the time I got to the aircraft I had trouble finding one which did not already have a pilot sitting in the cockpit. In vain I pleaded with Captain Thomas to let me fly as second pilot/gunner with Baron van der Linden d'Hoogvorst. He was adamant, and gave me a direct order to go back to barracks, pack up my kit and make my way to my squadron. By the time I had packed and was wondering what had happened at Le Zoute the news came through that the aircraft I had seen taking off that morning had been attacked just as they were landing. Rumour had it that there had been two killed and many others wounded, among

4

them being d'Hoogvorst with whom I had wanted to make the trip.

New orders sent me off to the railway station to get a train back to St. Trond via Brussels. In the capital there was an air of deathly quiet. Streets were deserted of traffic but small groups of people were on every corner, obviously talking and wondering what was happening. Parts of the city had already been bombed and I could see the ruin of the de Liedkerke hotel, one of the first buildings to be hit.

The train left the city and chugged steadily towards Liège. Between Tirlemont and Waremme I jumped from my seat when through the window I spotted a white-bellied Heinkel 111 flash across the landscape. At Liège I fell in with one of our squadron sergeants and we waited for a tram to continue our journey together. As we waited, a troop of Lancers on motor-cycles, tired-looking and covered with dust, came along the road, travelling fast. We could not understand why they were moving so fast *away* from the front line. We had no means of knowing the grim battle they had just gone through, thrown desperately in front of the advancing German armour and hopelessly outnumbered.

The tram came, we got aboard and it slowly ground its way out of town. A dozen times it was forced to stop whilst debris was cleared from the track. Finally we came to a dead stop in the open country; a bomb crater having put both the road and the tram track out of action. In the crater lay the remains of a small saloon car, still smoking. At the side of the road a tarpaulin had been thrown over the charred bodies of its former owners.

This sight, if nothing else, brought home to us the fact that we were now at war. Further along I saw more cars on their sides; houses gutted, their timbers stark and ugly against the sky. At Brusthem there were the remains of many of our CR42 aircraft destroyed by bombing.

We trudged along the road and were lucky enough to be overtaken by one of our Warrant-Officers in his car. We piled in among his cargo of corned beef and tobacco and learned something of what had been happening at St. Trond in our absence. We learned that our original base at Bierset had been heavily bombed. Stukas had destroyed more than twenty out of thirty of our fighters on an airstrip nearby. A sergeant pilot from one of our squadrons had been forced to bale out and was mistaken on the way down for a German parachutist and machine-gunned by our own troops.

At St. Trond we could see for ourselves what good use had been made of the trees around the perimeter. Camouflage was excellent and the mechanics had got the notion of changing it round twice a day as a further concealment. Even as I arrived on the airfield, a Henschel reconnaissance machine nosed down out of the clouds for a closer look but a well aimed burst of anti-aircraft fire sent him scurrying back up to cover. Next day we waited, with no orders to take off and no real news, only wild rumour. Then we learned that the Germans has crossed the Albert Canal. This meant they were only ten miles from us. Were we just to sit there and be captured without firing a shot? Then, in the middle of the afternoon we at last got firm orders to take-off. "Get the hell out of it quick!" was what the Cavalry Corps officer telephoning the order actually said. There was just time to tell us that our new base would be Steenokkerzeel when the line went dead. From St. Trond to Steenokkerzeel is only thirty-five miles but it was a trip I shall never forget.

Flying in open formation a thousand yards apart we saw the sky thick with JU87 Stukas and ME 109's strafing the Tirlemont road. We hugged the tree tops, so low that they did not see us. I recall the long black river of refugees along the country roads, fleeing to the roadside in panic every time an engine roared overhead. Louvain had been on fire for two days now and all I could see of the city was an enormous mushroom of black smoke through which we flew. Even in the cockpit I could taste the charred atmosphere and saw the smoke of the buildings wreathing round us as we flew through. Near Brussels a lone British Lysander aircraft crossed ahead going Heaven knows where. We gave him a friendly wave which the other pilot returned to us.

We were lucky. Eleven of our Renards got to Steenokkerzeel. The only one lost was attacked by three ME 109's just as it was taking off.

Landing at Steenokkerzeel the first thing we saw was the muzzle of a heavy anti-aircraft gun poking up over the hedge. It looked formidable and gave us something of a sense of security. In the evening we watched a long procession of British Army units moving up to positions near Louvain. They looked tough, professional soldiers and their equipment seemed modern and efficient. It was a comforting sight. We wondered if things were really as bad as people were saying. Surely it couldn't be true about a German break-through at Waremme?

At dawn, we had a noisy reveille when the anti-aircraft gun started firing. Didier and I were the crew on readiness and we were briefed on the airstrip. Then we learned about the capture in two days of what we had thought was the impregnable fort of Eben-Emael. Somebody said that the German gliders had landed on the roof of the fort itself but this we just could not believe. Across the airfield we could see more British units passing along in a steady stream and we wondered how they would manage to get through the crowds of refugees all struggling in the opposite direction.

An hour or two later Didier and I were stood-down from readiness alert but at lunch-time we were again warned for stand-by and this time were given a specific mission. We were to take-off and patrol the Quatrecht–St. Trond sector and reconnoitre enemy strength and positions for our Cavalry Corps opposing them.

On the way out to the aircraft Didier and I discussed how we would fly the mission. For both of us it would be our first operational flight in war and, although neither of us mentioned it, we both knew that our aircraft was slow, ill-armed, and easy meat for any ME 109 on the look out for just such a mission as ours. Were we frightened? Maybe we were but under such conditions you cannot really call it fright. This was our job; the one we had volunteered to do and I think our only worry was that we would be prevented from doing it. We were probably more frightened of failure than anything else. Climbing into the cockpit I suddenly remembered something one of my flying instructors had once said over the bar. 'A man who is not frightened by danger is only half a man but he who is frightened and keeps his fear under control is a hero.' At least we were heroic in that sense anyway!

The Renard lumbered across the grass and I eased back on the stick. As soon as I felt the control column between my hands a lot of my apprehensions vanished. Its hard, shiny feel was familiar and re-assuring. We flew low level, hugging the ground contours to Aarschot and passed over several

British units on the line of the Dyle and Demer rivers. Scanning the sky continually ahead I saw a speck in the sky over the Albert Canal and recognized it for a HE 111 on patrol. I lost height and orbited above the tree-tops watching him carefully. Although a bomber, he could fly almost a hundred miles an hour faster than me and had twice as much armament. Either by good luck or good camouflage we escaped the German crew's notice and I dived over Schaffen airfield, noting the Hurricanes which had been destroyed on the ground without firing a shot. How I wished I had had one of them under my hands—that HE 111 would not have continued making lazy orbits very much longer! Meanwhile Didier and I held a quick consultation and decided to start our mission from St. Trond towards Quatrecht. A few minutes later I saw troops on the road and realised from their uniforms that they were German. Some gazed up at us in surprise. Others did not wait and made a bee-line for the ditch. We noted their position and continued on course.

Suddenly I heard a flapping noise behind me and my first thought was that a safety strap had come loose. In turning I saw flashes of gunfire all along the Canal and realised it was light anti-aircraft fire. And aimed at us! I kicked hard left rudder, then right and zig-zagged through the sky with one eye on the tracer flashing up at an angle and the other on the tree-tops now dangerously close beneath the wing. There was a smell of burning but I could see no fire. Didier's voice became faint and I wondered if he had been hit. I opened the throttle wide and headed for home at the maximum speed the Renard could make, about 175 mph.

We landed intact and turning round I saw Didier was all right. Some intercom fault had made his voice fade away. He looked a bit pale and I do not suppose I was all that healthy looking myself. Still we had undergone our baptism of fire and completed our mission. So that was that!

I managed to get a few hours leave and a lift in a car to Brussels; only to find the house which was my home empty. A neighbour heard my knocking and told me that at lunchtime my parents had decided to leave the house. They did not know for where.

I got into the house, enjoyed the luxury of a bath and a real bed, and set my alarm for 2.15 am. The sergeant with whom I shared the lift had promised to collect me at the top of my street to go back together.

A few hours sleep and I was up and groping my way through the blacked-out street. Just as I reached the corner a soldier stepped out, pointed a rifle and sharp looking bayonet at me and asked for the password! I hadn't got a clue about any passwords and said so. This meant me being marched at bayonet point to the local guard commander who added his own revolver to the collection of armament aimed at me. It took a lot of talking and the timely arrival of the sergeant friend before we convinced them I was not a German parachutist in disguise.

The idea of a fifth column had made people jumpy and nervous. Everyone knew someone else who had seen German parachutists descending from the sky dressed as anything from bus conductors to nuns. Certainly at times dummies were dropped with devices fixed to them which fired off bursts of automatic fire in order to start panics; and sometimes they were very effective in doing just that.

The Squadron moved again, always falling back, to Grimbergen, and then Hemixen near Antwerp. The news got blacker and blacker. The Germans were across the Albert Canal and in control of the whole of its length. Louvain and Tirlemont had been occupied. Armoured units had broken through between Namur and Sedan and were reported racing across France.

On the 14th May, Brussels had been declared an open city. On the 17th the Germans entered it and a cousin of mine who was there at the time told me what it was like. "By the afternoon the streets were deserted. Not even a stray cat prowling about. Then, at about five o'clock two German soldiers on bicycles with rifles slung across their backs, pedalled slowly down the Avenue de Tervueren. They looked just like a couple of tourists trying to find their way. They were followed by a German staff car with the hood down with a cameraman standing up and filming away. And that is how the first German troops entered Brussels."

We still had our aircraft intact, mainly owing to the very good camouflage on the ground; an art at which we had by now become expert.

Another move, this time to St. Nicolas but the Intelligence

Section and two machines with their crews were ordered to stay behind at Hemixen. Didier and I, together with the other crew Adjudant Boel and Lieutenant Van der Beek then learned that we had to fly a reconnaissance mission behind enemy lines from Antwerp to Bilsen, then along the Albert Canal and return via the Escaut-Meuse Canal. We also learned that the last time this particular mission had been flown six aircraft had been lost from the squadron flying it!

Boel and van der Beek were ordered off first. Boel was cheerful but I noticed van der Beek carefully putting some odd pieces of steel sheet in the cockpit as makeshift protection.

After an hour of anxious waiting we heard the sound of an engine. It seemed somewhat sick; and finally our Renard staggered over the trees. What a mess! It had been hit so many times that Captain Lekeuche, our squadron commander, decided it was unrepairable and ordered it destroyed on the spot. Miraculously Boel and van der Beek were unhurt. The windscreen was shot clean away and another shell had passed millimetres from Boel's neck. Examination of van der Beek's steel sheets showed that he undoubtedly owed his life to them. Wise man!

At mid-day we got the order to pull out. The butler at the manor where we were billeted helped us to spend an hour more in a civilised environment and cooked us a lunch which I still remember with mouth-watering nostalgia. He topped it off by presenting us with a bottle of the best champagne in the cellar. What he did with the rest I never knew but I do know that the Germans never got it.

I took off at three in the afternoon and even as I opened the throttle I saw the ground crews setting fire to the wreck of Boel's aircraft. Then they scattered to their transport and wasted no time in getting away from there. Not until some of them arrived back at St. Nicolas did I learn that as I took off I had four ME 109's behind me! They must have mistaken me for a Henschel which had just bombed the airfield; the flames from Boel's Renard having helped to convince them. I think it was just about then I began to speculate that maybe I was born lucky!

That night we broached our precious bottle of champagne and toasted future victories. Some of us had to wait years for them. More of us never lived to see them.

A French tank unit with about a hundred tanks bivouacked down in the woods near us. They had been thrown into a counter-attack near Breda which had failed and their morale was pretty low to say the least. During the night they moved on south and we wondered if there was a chance of the big counter-offensive everyone was talking about.

Once again on the move. By now we were so mobile no one ever unpacked. We did not have much to unpack anyway. It only took an hour or so and again we were on the road or in the air. This time to an unknown spot on the map called Zwevezele between Courtrai and Bruges. There was the providential wood in which to hide our aircraft. On the 18th Didier and I flew a mission along the Scheldt from Ghent to Antwerp. As we followed the river we could everywhere see retreating troops and Germans obviously getting ready to cross the river. It was equally obvious that the amount of Belgian territory left to us was shrinking rapidly. Only our own troops fired on us but we forgave them because they had become so used to seeing only hostile machines in the sky that they automatically opened up at anything overhead within range.

Back in the Mess stories filtered through telling how other units had fared. We heard about the nine Belgian Fairey Battles sent to attack the Albert Canal bridges. Only three came back. The British too, suffered heavy losses attacking the same bridges with the same type of aircraft.

Landing back from a flight one of our Renards spun in and the observer was killed. The pilot had suddenly seen an aircraft diving on to him but it turned out to be a British Hurricane. Maybe the Hurricane pilot had made the same mistake in Renard/Henschel recognition which had saved me. Sadly the crashing plane fell on a number of our mechanics sleeping in the woods. They were all killed. What a tragically stupid waste of life!

Breyre, one of our pilots, was worried about his wife, nursing in a hospital at Coxyde and persuaded me to go with him that evening to find her. On the sea front at Coxyde we suddenly heard engines and looked up to see a Heinkel 111 with five RAF Hurricanes on his tail and queuing up to get at him. It was all over in thirty seconds. A rattle of gunfire, a couple of explosions and the Heinkel had crashed down to the sea. So at least the Luftwaffe was not having everything its own way.

11

On Sunday the 19th we were visited by Senior Staff Officers who congratulated us on 'the magnificent job you are doing.' We wondered if they were really serious! We had no illusions about our slow, inadequately equipped and armed aircraft. Despite that we flew our reconnaissance missions but had begun to wonder whether it was all worth while. For whom were we flying reconnaissance? Who was there to use whatever information we managed to bring back? Why did we not have faster, fighting type aircraft with cameras instead of what were little better than World War 1 machines and techniques?

Another reconnaissance mission, this time in the St. Nicolas area. We obtained what information we could and then located the small field west of Ghent which was the Divisional headquarters of the Infantry. We dropped our message container and looked for the white cloth strips being put out on the ground to acknowledge its receipt. These were the primitive methods we were still employing. The Army even had a strip combination which, de-coded, meant 'Enemy aircraft are attacking you'. By the time the pilot had deciphered this it wouldn't have mattered anyway!

When we landed back from this mission I thought our CO was a little effusive with his welcome. Not until later did we learn that two aircraft from our sister squadron had been shot down the day before flying the identical route. He had tactfully omitted to mention this to us in his pre-flight briefing!

Over the next day we saw more and more of our troops passing along the road. This time they were not coherent, disciplined fighting units. They seemed bunches of tired, worn-out and dispirited personnel, shambling to the rear. An army in retreat is not a happy sight and less so when it is one's own army. They had fought, and fought hard, but it was always the same story. Not enough men; not enough equipment and what they had was inferior to the German's modern weapons. Retreat had become the only possible course of action. They were ashamed, not of having been beaten but of not having been able to do more. They felt cheated and angry with themselves and with everyone else.

A sudden mysterious order out of the blue had us making test flights round the airfield with an overload. About the weight of three persons, in fact as we very soon calculated. Now what could this be for? We made a guess and I think we

were right. The Germans had now penetrated north of Abbeville and any hope of escape by road to the south was gone.
We were virtually in a bridgehead and might soon even be
surrounded. Indeed from all the rumours and counter-rumours
we heard that might even now be the case. So obviously the
extra weight which represented just two crew and one extra
without any kit must mean an air evacuation of the squadron
and its personnel.

We were able to do some good later by flying over the River
Lys sector looking for a gun battery which had been particularly
troublesome for our troops. It was thought to be somewhere in
the Waregem woods and the whole area was hazy with the
smoke from burning houses. Judging from the flashes on the
ground a considerable artillery duel was in progress. Just near
the woods we were met by a well aimed burst of anti-aircraft
fire. The explosions rocked the machine and I could smell the
cordite smoke whipping past in the slipstream. I dived and
dodged to port, then starboard. As I turned, the same battery
opened up again but now I had it spotted; and as soon as I saw
the flashes on the ground, side slipped violently away despite
Didier's protests that I was spoiling his search for the ground
artillery. He finally got the enemy battery pinpointed and we
put down the nose and hurtled home in a long dive to the airstrip. Happily our information helped the gunners to silence
the German battery within an hour or two.

That evening a Heinkel 111 in trouble, its starboard engine
smoking and useless, flew slowly over our airfield. The ground
gunners reacted too late and it escaped. We raged at this. If
only we had a better aircraft than our slow Renards. If only . . .
if, if, always 'if'. It put us all in a bad temper. Just to add to
our frustration a Heinkel 111 crashed just north of us later and
we went to examine it. We contrasted its strong metal construction with our own vintage fabric-covered machines. No wonder
we were losing!

A warning had come that we might be ordered to fly all our
seven remaining machines to England. With three aircrew in
each, that meant we could get over twenty-one aircrew away.
Hence the overload tests. If they could seriously plan and work
out a scheme like this then the end must be very near. In the
middle of our discussion, our Bierset sister-squadron flew in.
They were in even worse shape and only had three Renards left,

the other nine all having been destroyed in the air over the last few days. We reluctantly donated them one of ours.

That night German artillery found our airstrip and the occasional shell dropped among the trees and around the field. It was one in the morning when the order to pull out came through. We had a moment of hope that it might, after all, be to England so that we could re-equip and fight on. But it was only as far as the river Yser near the coast on an improvised strip made from the former golf course at Lombarzyde. Even as I took off, several shells burst on the far side of the field; and flying west through the dark we saw fires everywhere on the ground. It is a terrible feeling to see one's country literally burning up beneath one and be unable to do anything about it.

There was some mix-up with an airfield construction unit about marking out our landing strip and they put white stripes in the wrong place. We did not know it as we came in. The first machine got down, bouncing crazily along. The second mis-judged his approach and overshot finishing up among the dunes farther along. I came in all right and touched down where the surface seemed good. Then the Renard lurched violently to one side, there was a splintering of wood, and she careered round almost in a ground loop as one undercarriage leg dug deep into an unseen hole. No. 9 Squadron strength was now down to four.

Above us stretched a long, black cloud. This was the smoke from burning Dunkirk. Someone reported that Germans had been seen in the Zeebrugge area. The bridgehead was now down to but a few miles perimeter. It was, although we did not realise it, the last day of our Battle for Belgium.

Monday 27th May, like many of those in the last ten days, was sunny and cloudless. Free of normal, Heaven-sent clouds that is. The long black, obscene looking cloud trailing across the sky all that day was man-made from the fires of war. In and out of it aircraft dodged; swooped down, then back up to disappear through the greasy smoke. We could hear the drone of the Dorniers and JU87's heading for the Dunkirk beaches and hear the screams of their engines in the dive, followed by the flat thump of the bombs. Above the cloud, engines whined and roared as the Hurricanes and Spitfires fought through the ME109's to get at the bombers. I believe that when the British Army came back from Dunkirk they were asking bitterly where

the RAF was at the time. I could have told them. The noise of
their guns came down to us and every now and then a smoking
silhouette would come hurtling straight down from above the
black mass and plunge straight into the ground. Sometimes
you could see the black cross on it but sometimes, too, it was a
red, white and blue roundel.

I had been ordered to survey the beach to see if we could land
a Sabena civil passenger plane on it in order to pull out squadron
personnel. Pacing along the shore we saw a Heinkel 111
suddenly peel off and dive on to our airfield. The bombs fell
in a straight stick, one, two, three, four and the fourth one
exploded only a hundred yards from me. Our last four aircraft
were safe but the strip was unusable from then on. The Heinkel
had been able to take his time and carry out a text-book
bombing run. I don't know if it was the same HE111 I saw
later spiral down out of control with a Hurricane on his tail.
Probably not. The Germans seemed to have hundreds of them
in the sky over Belgium.

That night we were bombed in our billets by Dornier 217's.
I awoke to an almighty crash and my bed seemed to take off
and hang in the air. I hurried downstairs and was met at the
foot by a solemn-faced Didier. He didn't say much but his
face told me the news.

"Capitulation?"

He nodded, too emotionally numb to speak.

Still we could not believe it. In the operations room no one
seemed to know what was happening. "Stay put", was all that
higher command could tell us. Didier and I went to one side
and quietly discussed the chances of getting away, maybe to
England, with one of the remaining Renards. We decided to
go down and look them over. Over to one side I saw a German
bomber dive on to the Nieuport bridges and drop bombs. That
seemed to give the lie to the capitulation story. Then, as he
climbed away three Hurricanes pounced on him. He dived
back to ground level and never in my life before or since have I
seen such a low flying performance as that Luftwaffe pilot
put on. He threw his Dornier 17 round the trees like a fighter
and finally shook off the Hurricanes. Looking back on it now
I suppose I can say good luck to him but on that day I was
wishing I could hear the Hurricanes guns blast him out of the
sky.

We saw a car on its way to the airstrip but did not know that it was one of our officers with orders to put the Renards permanently out of action. In the operations room there were, at last, firm orders. They were explicit. 'The fighting is over. Anyone attempting to leave will be court-martialled for desertion.' Despite this Didier and I discussed a makeshift plan for obtaining one of the many small cabin cruisers moored in the Yser estuary and getting away.

We were forestalled by another order, this time to make our way back to Tirlemont for demobilisation. In what lorries we had left we formed up into a convoy and headed for Tirlemont. Several times on the way we stopped to let German motorized columns, trucks packed with troops, armoured cars and, overhead, patrolling aircraft pass by. They ignored us. Speed was their problem; we could wait.

That evening we camped out in a small village, miserable in a damp drizzle which had set in. No one talked much. No one wanted to. We smoked our last cigarettes and drank our last bottles of beer.

I confessed to our CO the plans Didier and I had been making.

"And where," he asked gloomily, "would you have gone?"

"England", we said. He shook his head.

"Useless. Nothing can stop these columns. You see. It's only a matter of weeks now before the end."

The effect of his prophecy was somewhat spoiled the next moment when three Blenheims dropped out of the overcast sky and deposited a load of bombs on a nearby crossroads.

Frans Breyre, van der Beek and myself were detailed to take a car and proceed ahead to Tirlemont as advance party. We used Breyre's Ford, an ancient 1932 model. The roads were choked with the human tide of a defeated nation. Soldiers, some in compact groups, others in loose mobs were jammed in with civilians returning home, all wondering what they would find when they got there. Only a few bridges over the main rivers were open and the Germans were using these as convenient filters to segregate military from civilian personnel.

At a crossroads a German sentry shouted directions at us but, following them, we spotted barbed wire and turned away quickly. Heading for the River Lys we got entangled in an enormous jam of people, vans, carts and more people. It was

Left: **Renard 31 (Rolls-Royce Kestrel) in flight**

Below: **Renard Aircraft of 9 Squadron Belgian Air Force, lined up at Bierset Airfield in early '38**

Above: **Fairey Fox, equipped with a 850 HP Hispano engine, as flown by Lt Divoy**

Below Left: **Fiat CR 42 fighter (early 1940)**
Below right: **Gloster Gladiator**

Above: **Fairey Firefly in flight**
Below: **Fairey Battle, RR Merlin engine**
Above right: **Koolhoven trainer—used in 1940**
Below right: **Renard 36 fighter (RR Merlin) which crashed during trials, 1939**

Above: **Lacap bomber (prototype 1938)**

Above: **3 engine Fokker transport aircraft**

Above: **SV 5 trainer used until 1940**
Below: **Morane 230 aerobatic trainer**

Left: **Hurricane fighter which force-landed after being shot up in March 1940**

Below left: **British Hurricane which force-landed in Belgium a few hundred yards from the French border (pilot got away into France) winter '39-40**

Battle for Belgium, 1940. Fairey Foxes set on fire by the rear gunner of a Dornier 17

Top far left: **First Hurricane assembled in Belgium, 1940**

Middle: **British Battle shot down in Belgium.**

Top right: **A Spitfire, Dewoitine 520 destroyed on an airfield in Northern France in 1940**

Bottom far left: **Ju52 troop transport shot down over Belgium, 1940**

Bottom right: **Renard reconnaissance aircraft in flight**

Below: **Pilots of 9 Squadron in 1940. Author is second from left**

Above right: **The home-made keys used to get into the hangar**

350 Squadron returns from an operation

Above right: **Mike Donnet with Baron and Baronne T. d'Huart, owners of the Stampe, when it was returned to them after the war**

Middle right: **Divoy's do-it-yourself instrument panel. The alarm clock is top right**

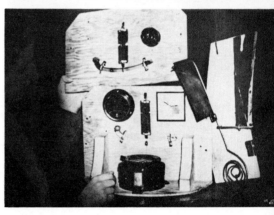

Below: **The author in the Stampe SV4 after his escape. Both now wear RAF uniform**

Above left: **Belgians in 609 Squadron on the wing Flt Lt Offenberg, Fg Off de Spirlet, Fg Off de Selys Longchamps, Plt Off C. Ortmans, Sergeant R. Lallemant, Plt Off Wilmet**

Below left: **Belgian Pilots in 64 Squadron, 1942—Flt Lt Prevot, Plt Off Mertens, Plt Off Divoy, Plt Off Donnet**

Above right: **Mike Donnet in the Spitfire IX 'Francqui' Hornchurch, summer 1942**

Left: **Plt Off Prune, one of the originals drawn by Bill Hooper, familiar to all World War II aircrew**

Above: **Bill Crawford-Compton, CO of 64 Squadron, in front of his Spitfire, 'The Magic Carpet' (Fairlop early 1943)**

Below: **'Junior' Harder and Hancock 'testing' a new transport mode**

wedged immoveable, waiting for the bridge to be opened. Breyre put the Ford across country and the gallant old car bounced and jolted along over the fields. A few hundred yards from the bridge we came to a dead stop and could get no farther. Breyre went ahead on foot and came back a few minutes later grinning. He had found the top Air Force Staff group who were making their way through and with a German staff car to lead them and clear the way. We literally manhandled the old Ford through the jam and tagged on to the end of the VIP Convoy. This time it was plain sailing behind the big staff cars ahead. We crossed the bridge. Beyond it the roads were quiet and deserted.

Near Alost one of the rear tyres went. This gave us problems. If we stopped to fix it we would lose the party we were tagged on to. If not, we might not be able to keep up. We decided to chance it and bounced and rattled along with the tyre in shreds, running on the wheel rim. Luckily the convoy stopped for a halt and gave us time to get the spare wheel on.

It was midnight when we reached Brussels. Most of the canal bridges had been blown up and sentries were guarding the temporary bridges flung across by German engineers. Not a soul stirred in the streets. We quickly decided that staying with our top-brass convoy might be all very well and had got us on our way but would inevitably lead to a prisoner-of-war compound. We decided to part company and passing the main station, Breyre switched off his lights and we veered off down a side street. He said he knew a hotel which might still be open and in business. It was, with lights on and we just took the German sentry in the lounge as some piece of new officialdom we would have to get used to. We booked a couple of rooms, went upstairs and enjoyed the luxury of a hot bath. Then into bed.

We could not have been asleep more than an hour when there was a pounding on the door and an anxious proprietor appealing to us to come down. It appeared there had been a mistake and we were in a German Officer's Mess. Was Breyre's face ever red!

Instead of a sprung bed we finished the night on mattresses in the German Guard room. In the morning they told us to report to the Caserne Albert, a military barracks near the town centre. A civilian interpreter had to go along as well and since

17

there was not enough room in the car I volunteered to stay behind.

Breyre came back for me and, meanwhile, a Luftwaffe NCO pilot who had drifted into the guardroom on some mysterious errand, told the guard corporal that he was going to the Caserne and would escort us. At the top of the Boulevard Botanique he made Breyre stop the car, stated that he had never any intention of going anywhere near the Caserne, slapped us both on the back, wished us luck and disappeared. In this way he had given us a chance to get away.

We couldn't take it. Breyre had told van der Beek we would be back and so round to the Caserne we had to go. In the court-yard of the Caserne there was a long line of officers all waiting to have their details taken down by several perspiring German clerks. No one seemed to know what was happening and we noticed that behind us armed sentries were stopping anyone going back out the way we had come in. Breyre and I looked at each other then both turned about and, side-by-side and in step, we marched out through the gate. The German sentries never gave us a second glance!

We soon got back home to Stockel and changed into civilian clothes, had a shave and some food and felt a lot better. Then we went out to explore. It was enough for me when I saw the Nazi flag floating over the Royal Palace and I came home feeling miserable and angry. A neighbour told us he had heard that the Germans would soon close all roads except for anyone with official passes. Breyre wanted to get home to Liège. He still had the car and I decided to go with him. I made up my mind about this because I had remembered the previous night something someone, somewhere, had told me not long before. It was that there was a factory near Liège in whose warehouse one or two privately owned aircraft had been stowed away before the main German attack. I very much wanted to know if this were true.

We drove along deserted roads and through silent villages. In the ditches there was the flotsam of war, burned-out vehicles, kit, steel helmets and clothing. It was depressing and ugly. The Maas bridges had been blown but a ferry was in service and we decided to chance it. Luck had held so far. Perhaps it would still hold.

It didn't. An inquisitive German 'Feldpolizei' ferreted around the car and uncovered our uniforms. At the door of the citadel he formally commandeered our faithful old Ford in the name of the Third Reich and handed us over to the guard room. The huge door clanged shut behind us and we were inside . . .

3

In the Bag

The night of the 1st June, 1940, precisely twenty-one days
after our war started, Breyre and I were prisoners-of-war in a
makeshift compound established in a deserted porcelain
factory. The next night we were two of sixty brother officers
crammed into a third class railway carriage grinding over
points and sleepers northwards. We ended up in a tented camp
erected in woods, not exactly sure of our whereabouts but
quite certain that it was a long way from home. The camp
looked peaceful enough and the sky was blue with white
clouds floating across it. But if you looked down and not up
you saw barbed wire and watch-towers; the guards in them with
wicked-looking Schmeissers cradled in one arm. It was the
sight of that wire which really brought home to me that I had
lost man's most valuable possession, his freedom. I looked up at
the sky, back at the wire and there and then decided I had not
lost it . . . just temporarily put it to one side. I would take it
up again when I was good and ready.

Again we were herded into trains. Cattle trucks this time.
We rattled and bounced along all that day and part of the next.
The Germans still talked about us all being set free once
"formalities were complete" but we noticed that all the time
we were travelling east. This journey ended in a newly built
army camp near Soest in Westphalia. Here we met up again
with many people we had not seen for weeks. Among others I
spotted Didier and we shook hands with some feeling. After
Westende he had disappeared and made his way along the
coast but was captured. That was far from the end for Lieutenant Didier. He was to live to make no less than thirteen
attempts to escape and each time was re-captured.

Yet again we were put on the move, this time to Dortmund.
This set the pattern for the next seven months during which time

20

the Germans moved us from Dortmund to Nuremberg; to Frankfurt; Cassel; Trèves and finally Metz. I became used to soup made from mangel-wurzels and fish; and sausages made with paper! Bread was made from bran and tea from briar roots. I got to know hunger well. I saw it do strange things to men. I saw a soldier try and trick his way to the top of the soup queue and saw his angry fellow-prisoners take hold of him and throw him bodily in the vat. Then I saw others scraping the sticky stuff off his clothes and on to their own plates.

The German treatment varied with each camp. Sometimes they were humane, easy-going and all for a quiet life. At other places they were typical Nazi bullies. It all depended on who-ever was in charge. All ranks took their cue from the top.

We spent a lot of time keeping out of the way and evading the drafting for forced labour in Germany which was going on. I say with shame that although most of my countrymen thought the same as me, I know of some who were only too eager to get into Germany to work for the Germans in return for the extra creature comforts they were offered.

We thought constantly of escape and I had several plans. I had a chance or two; especially once on the line between Frank-furt and Bad Orp during an air raid. However I reasoned that if I were caught I would be sent to a special prisoner fortress and since news from other camps seemed to indicate that Belgian prisoners were being released anyway it did not seem worth it without a much better plan.

At Trèves there were some British prisoners. They incurred the fury of the German guards one night when, during an air raid, they opened the windows of their barrack huts and sang 'Tipperary' at the top of their voices.

The last move to Metz gave us some hope. At least we were back in France and not in Germany any longer. On the 9th January it was once again into the cattle trucks for yet another move. Where to? By now we were past caring. In the train were over two hundred Belgians and among them, a dozen French soldiers whom de Lannoy, my prison-camp companion, and I had quietly managed to smuggle into the trucks with us. Cold, hungry and fed-up we dozed the night through and at six in the morning, when the train stopped in a station, someone poked his nose through the bars and asked a porter where we were.

His reply electrified us. It was Arlon! At last we were back in Belgium! Cold and hunger forgotten we stood to attention and sang the "Brabanconne" our national anthem. The train stopped again further on and we were allowed to get out and stretch our legs. Some of the men fell down and, emotionally overcome, kissed the ground. People came from lineside cottages and gave us hot coffee and there was much hand-shaking and not a few tears.

The train pulled up with a final hiss of steam and grinding of brakes under the great glass roof of Antwerp central station. We walked through the barrier, received our discharge papers from the German military police and passed out into the street free men. Free? Well, no longer prisoners-of-war and no longer military personnel. Let me qualify that. Perhaps we did not wear uniform but in the minds of many of us we were still at war and determined to carry on fighting against the invader in our own way. That was one order no one had any need to put into writing.

I caught a later train to Brussels and went to the famous Bon Marché store. A welfare centre for servicemen back from prison-camps had been established whose purpose was to turn us, outwardly at least, into some semblance of respectable civilians again and to provide any facilities they could in the way of messages to home. And it was just as I was leaving that I came into my first contact with that new, strange and dangerous underworld just then beginning to grow in secrecy throughout occupied Europe. Passing one of the counters a saleswoman put out a hand and stopped me.

"Army?" she asked. I shook my head.

"No. Air Force. Pilot," I said.

She looked round carefully and then brought her head closer. It was quite a pretty head too.

"Pilots are needed in England" she whispered. "When you decide to go, come and see me. Ask for Simone."

I walked out pondering and suddenly felt renewed hope. So whatever I planned to do I wouldn't be on my own. Maybe there was help waiting. Maybe some unknown someone had a good plan all cut and dried. Well, I could undoubtedly find out soon.

22

4

Hope and Despair

My homecoming was made on a good old Brussels tramcar, swaying and grinding through familiar streets and past all the old landmarks. Every road crossing was a milestone from what seemed like years ago. The arch of the Cinquantenaire; our old college of St. Michael; the park of Woluve . . . they were all there little changed and each full of memories for me. I got off the tram at Stockel and then through the familiar gate. It still squeaked. That day started in the cold morning mist of Metz and ended in a riot of welcoming cries, hugs, kisses and tears.

For a few days I rested and lapped up home life again. I got used to the rationed bread like sticky, grey paste and quickly learned how the ordinary people managed to survive on a starvation diet. Once I had to visit the Kommandantur to get some stamp or other on my release papers. An officious young Leutnant went into a screaming fit at me because I should apparently have handed in my uniform. God knows why he wanted it. Maybe to count and record the fleas! Anyway so long as I could hang on to it I was determined that no German would get his hands on it.

The next task was that of finding a job. Someone put me in touch with the 'Winter Help' organisation who occupied themselves supplying extra food and fuel to those in real need. I applied for an administrative job in the local office and a week after my return they said I could start.

During that week I had seen old friends from the Air Force days and we met together in ones and twos to swap the latest news. It would have been dangerous to have gathered in larger groups. The watchful eye of the Gestapo was everywhere, so they told me, and half-a-dozen or more known ex-officers meeting together would have been enough for them to pounce. Word was trickling through about those of our comrades who had got away and were in England. We heard that de Cannart d'Hamale, whom we had all known well at flying school, had been killed in combat, flying with the Royal Air Force. We arranged a memorial service for him but there were not many of us able to be there. I thought afterwards that we should have worn uniform and mounted a guard of honour. That would have given the Germans something to think about.

Stories of escapes flew around from mouth to mouth over café tables and in the corners of city bars. They said two complete football teams had been picked up by a JU52 to fly to a match in Germany but instead had altered course and ended up in England. The 'players' were all would-be escapers.

One of my friends, Robert Voss, was full if plans and hints for escaping. I believed everything he told me. I wanted to believe it! Heady talk of this and that certain way of getting across; the tip from the shopgirl in the Bon Marché. Oh yes! It wouldn't be long now.

More than once Voss telephoned me agitatedly and warned me to be ready at such-and-such-a-place and named a time but on each occasion the arrangements fell through. In the last week of March, Voss contacted me yet again. This time it was for certain. To be ready on the Friday night with photographs, identity card and fifteen hundred francs. Nothing could go wrong!

All that evening and half the night I spent waiting at home in eager anticipation. Every sound on the street made me jump up but morning came and still no Voss. I went reluctantly to work and had not been there long when my brother telephoned and said someone at home wanted to see me. I jumped on my bicycle and pedalled madly back. Waiting in the hall was a little man who leaned towards me with a confidential air and said that Voss had sent him. He thereupon produced from a brief case a long string of pink sausages! Explanations were due and I learned that my little man ran a profitable line in black market sausages; but whilst it was true that Robert Voss had recommended him to call at our house it was another man and not the one I was expecting. Anyway the sausages tasted very good.

In April my old friend Divoy, whom I had fully thought was already in England, telephoned me. On the telephone he was cautious and non-committal. You had to be. He simply said he was in Brussels, hadn't seen me for a long time and what about meeting for a drink?

We arranged to meet in the Gargantua bar and I went to keep the appointment with anticipation. I knew my Divoy. He hadn't telephoned me just for a social drink. Over two weak and watery beers he confirmed my suspicions. He had a plan and wanted to talk it over with me.

"We're both pilots," he said. "So why not take to our natural element?"

"You mean fly out?" I asked wonderingly.

"But where? . . . I mean how? . . . An aircraft? . . ."

Divoy raised his glass and under cover of its rim gave me a sly wink.

"We build one," he said.

"O.K. We build one. Now you tell me how we get the parts? Buy them second-hand from the Luftwaffe?"

"Look," he said. "I live in the Ardennes on a farm. You know where. It's pretty remote and the Germans never come round. There's plenty of timber and somewhere to work. I've already roughed out a plan of the airframe."

"Engine?" I asked.

"All organised. I've got a big Gnome and Rhone twin-cylinder hidden away. Not much but should be enough to get two of us airborne and well on the way. All I need is a propeller."

"Is that all?" I said.

We agreed a propeller was a problem and finished our beers wondering about it. I went back home and Divoy went on somewhere else after promising to keep in touch.

That evening the phone rang again and it was Divoy. He sounded excited.

"I'm coming round right now," he said. "I think I've got what we want."

He could hardly wait to get inside the door before telling me his news. It seemed that by an amazingly lucky chance, after leaving me he had run into Elie d'Ursel, another old pilot friend of ours. Divoy had hinted to him that a small oddment such as a serviceable propeller might come in handy and apparently d'Ursel knew exactly where such a thing could be had.

"Not only that" said Divoy excitedly. "There's something more."

"How much more?"

He grinned and slapped my back.

"It seems this propeller might ... it just might ... be attached to a complete, fully serviceable, ready-to-fly aeroplane !"

I sat down and considered this bombshell.

"O.K." I said at last. "What's the catch ?'

"No catch. You remember d'Ursel's cousin. The one who was CO of a fighter squadron ? Well, he had a small private aircraft of his own and when war started he had it stowed away on an estate in the Forest of Soignes. It's at Terbloc, the Chateau of Thierry d'Huart."

I knew the place vaguely. It wasn't far away. An easy three-hour cycle ride there and back.

"So how do we find out if it's still there ?"

"We go and see, stupid !"

The first day I could get off I organised an innocent cycle outing. There was my young brother Mark and a couple of his friends, the Valcke brothers; and myself. We headed for the forest in the direction of Terbloc and pedalled steadily for an hour or two. It was quiet and the road deserted. As we went along my spirits rose. What if there should be a fine, lovely aircraft just waiting for someone to come along and liberate it ? There would be problems, of course. Would there be room to take-off ? What about fuel ? Details, details ! In my mind I brushed them aside. The machine was the thing.

No sooner had I reached this pleasant state of mental euphoria when I was brought down to earth with a bump. At the junction of the Namur and Malines roads not only was there a barrier preventing further movement through the forest but a fully-armed German guard to see the restriction was observed.

We were local boys and knew the forest like the back of our hands. We pedalled on happily south because we knew that a little further along there was a handy lane leading to our destination.

Shock number two! Another steel-helmeted armed guard on duty at the gate of the Chateau. We kept on pedalling past. Obviously the Germans were using the Chateau. This would make things tricky. Very tricky indeed.

Farther along the lane we dumped our bicycles in the hedge and crawled through it. We were at the rear of the house and in a good spot from which to see the large field sloping gently away to the forest. At the far edge of the field was a hollow and

26

in the hollow a wooden building which looked like a hangar. Anyway if there was an aircraft here that was the most likely place for it to be.

Leaving the Valcke brothers on guard over the bicycles, Mark and I walked cautiously round in the shadow of the hedge until we had reached a point opposite the hangar. From here on, was an open field and we crawled across carefully, taking advantage of every fold in the ground.

When I think back to that day my hair curls at realisation of the risk we took. It needed only an alert sentry or some German out for a stroll to have spotted us and not only would all hope of aerial escape be gone for ever but we would both likely have been en route to a forced labour camp in double quick time. At the best, that is. At the worst a couple of quick shots for being on enclosed military premises might have answered just as well and that would have been that!

Fortune favours the brave, they say. I don't know if we were brave or just reckless but anyway we made it without being seen. Suddenly, before I could stop him, Mark had jumped up and was at the door, his eye to the join.

"Come back, you damn fool!" I hissed. Then I realised he had more sense than I gave him credit for. If he had been seen and arrested a young 17-year-old would have much more chance of being believed that it was just idle curiosity which had taken him to the shed than if he turned out to be an ex-Air Force pilot.

Mark came back, his face glowing. He flopped down beside me and squeezed my arm. "It's there!" He almost shouted it. "Complete! Engine, wings, wheels, tail, the lot!"

Cycling back to town, in our minds we were already airborne. Our cycles had wings. Or at least that's what it felt like.

Divoy had to be told. We met in the Winter Help vegetable store to which only I had the key. There, by candle-light and sitting on bundles of leeks and turnips I told him all about it.

"Obviously we have to give it a thorough inspection," he said.

"Slight problem," I pointed out. "Apart from the sentries and guards, the doors are padlocked. Don't suppose d'Ursel has a key?"

"Not very likely. We'll just have to have a look and make one to fit."

Again I shudder in retrospect to think what we contemplated

so lightheartedly. Armed guards, sentries, an occupying army and we decided we would just go there and take lock patterns to make a key. No trouble at all. Just like that! Maybe that's the difference between youth and middle-age.

At sunset the next Saturday, Mark and I set off once again. It was a blustery, wet and cloudy night which suited us admirably. The sort of night when sentries stay in the shelter of walls as long as they can. We hid our bicycles in the same place and followed the line of dripping trees round the field before cutting straight across to the hangar. Under cover of a coat which Mark held round my head and shoulders I switched on a small torch and made careful notes of the padlock, following the instructions which Divoy had given me before we left. I could not resist shining the torch through the crack in the woodwork and there was just enough light to let me see the gleam of a doped surface and what might have been a flying wire.

We were back before curfew and still had time to give Divoy the details I had gathered. By then he had found out that the machine was a Stampe SV4. That night I went up to the attic and dug out all the copies of old aviation magazines I had kept. Finally I found an article giving a good description of the Stampe. It had a speed of 110 knots and an endurance of three hours twenty minutes. Excellent! Just what we would need.

A few nights later Divoy and I were again pedalling towards Terbloc. By now my parents were getting a bit worried about these nocturnal outings. I told them some story about evening bike rides to keep fit but you can't fool parents for long and I think they both suspected that I was 'up to something'. They also suspected it was something the Germans would not approve of and it might mean trouble for me and hence for the whole family.

This time Divoy and I had cause for some bad language. Whether it was my draughtsmanship or his fitting ability the keys we had made were too large and would not fit.

We spent a few days filing away and on the 17th April paid our next visit. By now the route was as familiar to us as our own back garden but we dare not relax. The Chateau was only three hundred yards away and sometimes we could hear voices coming across the grass from open windows. We had brought our files and after half-an-hour's experiment, managed to get the padlock open.

Now, was there some sort of alarm system on the doors? Surely the Germans must know what was in the hangar and would have taken precautions to safeguard such valuable contents? No. That didn't follow. If they had known about the aircraft surely they would have taken it away before now. We felt all round the doors but found nothing. Well, staring at the doors would not open them. Here goes . . .

Gently we eased one of the doors back. It was stiff and with every squeak we held our breath, ready to run. Surely someone must hear us? No movement across the field, no shouts or flashlights or running feet. With a final heave and what sounded like an ear-splitting crash the door was fully open. We dived for the bushes and lay there for fifteen minutes before venturing out again. Everything was quiet and we slipped into the shed.

The Stampe was there! Covered in dust but very much there and, as far as we could see by our small torch, complete and in one piece. I patted it lovingly. The ailerons creaked when I moved the stick; the two tyres were flat as pancakes and the fuel tank was bone dry. There was no dashboard and instruments. But these were small setbacks we could surely overcome. The main things were all there. Engine, wings, just as Mark had said.

Back home there was a lot to be done. Much coming and going and following-up of clues after discreet and careful enquiries. I got hold of a gallon of petrol with which to check for fuel leaks.

Divoy undertook to make a new instrument panel. On a friend's tip-off he went to a warehouse in the port of Antwerp where he found a serviceable compass which had "fallen off the back of a lorry" assisted by Divoy's contact. A chemist friend made curved glass tubes which he filled with a coloured liquid. This gave us a simple but practical turn-and-bank indicator and an attitude indicator. It would also be a rudimentary artificial horizon for cloud use or at night. He found an old, oil-pressure gauge in a garage next door to his house. I scrounged various tools from here and there and, not the least important, some sandpaper to clean the plug points and contact breakers. There was an old motor-cycle silencer we thought might be useful and we added this to our collection.

We were at Terbloc again a week later. This time we got safely inside the hangar and measured up the gap where the instruments would have to go. We checked the fuel pipes, took a sample of the oil, still in the engine, and had a general look and check round to see if there was anything else we would have to make or scrounge. This took us a couple of hours and we had to pedal back pretty fast to get home before curfew at 11 o'clock that night.

Divoy worked like mad the next few days making the instrument panel and mounting our makeshift instruments. Like all maestros, he could not resist a final, finishing touch and mounted in one corner an alarm clock which he had been given years before as a confirmation present.

Our final, and biggest obstacle was finding twenty-five gallons of petrol. This really was a problem. Petrol was very strictly rationed and controlled but if one knew where to look there was always a little to be had. And a little it had to be each time so as to avoid suspicion. Nor could we buy even small quantities too frequently since people might start wondering or, even worse, talking. I finally decided to ask the help of my old friend Robert Voss and the Valcke brothers, who had been on our first reconnaissance, and between us we managed a pint here, and a bottle-full there.

Six days later we were in the hangar again. This time the weather was at its worst. Worst for anyone out in it but best for us. We worked in our socks to avoid leaving too many muddy marks and for silence. I pumped up the tyres and checked the magnetos. I climbed up on to the mainplane and carefully poured a precious gallon of petrol . . . siphoned off from a car . . . into the tank. We took out the plugs, cleaned them and poured a few drops of petrol into each cylinder before replacing the plugs.

Working in silence, making signs to each other we checked that the magneto switches were off and then, grasping one propeller blade firmly, I heaved on it and turned the engine over. God knew when it had last been turned! It seemed to be making a hell of a squeaking and grinding noise. Then I realised that this was because of the completely dry state of the engine, all the oil having drained down. Once she fired, and the oil was flowing, she would be all right. I kept heaving at the propeller whilst Divoy checked the spark at the contact breaker and the plugs. They worked. We checked and tightened a couple of oil lines and everything seemed O.K.

30

Our main problem was still a supply of fuel. Twenty-five gallons of it. Then, as we had always optimistically hoped, something turned up and from a most unexpected source. The Valcke brothers came round one night bursting with their news.

"Much as you want," they said. "Pricey, though." They named the price and we raised our eyebrows but were in no position to haggle. Especially when we learned where it would come from. The brothers almost choked with laughter when they told us.

"It's . . . it's a German Feldwebel at Evere. He's selling Luftwaffe aviation fuel on the black market!" How very, very appropriate! We liked it. We really did. What's more, para- doxically enough, it was the safest source we could have found. If a German were selling it he would be the last one to give us away since he would be the first to suffer. The German auth- orities had very strict regulations about things like that among their own ranks. And pretty severe punishments for anyone they caught at it too.

Only one more matter remained to be settled, this time between Divoy and me. We settled it in the "Gargantua" by tossing a coin.

"Heads," I said. It came down tails. That meant Divoy would act as pilot. Somehow I had hoped it would be me but anyway the Stampe had dual controls. Then with a slight shock we both realised that all we now needed to do was name the day and time. Recapitulating over the past month or two we could hardly believe that we had managed to get so far in so short a time. We had turned a wild dream into a distinct and practical possibility. A hundred things could have gone wrong, but miraculously none of them had. We decided that the weather rather than the time was the important thing. It would have to be a cloudy day so that we could fly to the coast in cloud on instruments and then slide in low over the North Sea and the English coast at low-level. That same afternoon I bought a Michelin road map on which we marked our intended route. We knew there were plenty of airfields in the Cambridge area and this would be our planned destination. The only news sources we had were German and we had got the impression that the whole of south-east England had been devastated and that landing would be difficult.

31

Getting the petrol to Terbloc was a problem but we finally solved it by obtaining four cans and splitting them up between my brother, Mark, Robert Voss and the Valcke brothers, one to each bicycle. We were all set. It all depended on the weather now. Naturally there ensued a spell of cloudless skies and bright sunlight! We held another 'briefing' and decided that a night take-off and flight would be safer and offer us a better chance. Thus we could now fix a day, or rather a night; and we promptly fixed it for the 19th May. I worked it out that we had to get the aircraft out of the hangar before sunrise. Say two hours and forty-five minutes before at the earliest, and with one hour as safety margin. We had to be airborne, at the very latest, one hour ten minutes before first light.

So there we were. A night take-off from a small field at the back of a house full of German soldiers; in an aircraft which had not flown for years and with an engine which had not run for as long; with home-made rudimentary instruments and nothing but darkness to protect us. It was all quite mad and quite impossible and only had one chance in a hundred of coming off. So we were mad and the idea preposterous, yet we went on with it. Why? If you have ever lived in an occupied country and seen that country overwhelmed and crushed in days; if you know what it is to wake at night in fear for the sound of a car engine outside or a knock on the door; if you eke out a daily existence by permission of a steel-helmeted, armed and jack-booted totalitarian authority; if you have known all these things you will understand why we went on with it. If you have never known these things you can only guess and call us mad.

Our petrol carrying team were to meet at my uncle's house in the next street. This was where we had our concealed fuel dump. Each would load a five-gallon can on his bike and all set off together to rendezvous later. Divoy and I would walk, since for us it was a one-way trip this time. We put on our uniforms under mackintoshes; and I unearthed our old Service revolvers from their hiding place.

At dinner the whole family was tense. There was no doubt about it that by now my parents had guessed almost all of what was going on. I pushed away my plate, went upstairs, changed into my uniform and the mackintosh, then came quietly down. At the foot of the stairs the whole family were waiting. They

were telling me to stay and I could see tears in my sisters'
eyes. I was deeply moved. They were all very brave. Braver
than I; for if anything went wrong they too would suffer just
for being my family.

At the corner I met Divoy and we started our tramp. It was
a mild spring evening. We both carried suitcases with what
small kit we could pack plus the instrument panel and the
engine silencer. We marched along in silence, each busy with
our thoughts.

Deep in the forest, halfway along a forestry road, Divoy
suddenly put a hand on my arm and we stopped. Then I heard
it. The heavy tramp of feet somewhere behind us. It seemed to
be just one man and soon we spotted him. It was a German
soldier! With our raincoats in warm weather and suitcases we
were very suspicious-looking but we strolled on, trying to
look like a couple of nature lovers out for a ramble. Our man
stayed the same distance behind and made no effort to quicken
his pace. At the Quatre-Bras he turned off and we breathed
again. Maybe he was a nature-lover too!

It was dusk and after two hours walking we were relieved
when we got to the rendezvous to see the others waiting there.
They had not encountered any real trouble. Only once when
some young Luftwaffe men had heard the cans jolting on the
back of the bikes and run alongside making jokes about 'bone-
shakers' and 'any old iron'. However this was just to impress
the girls they were with to raise a giggle and they soon gave it
up.

We reached the edge of the field behind the house and here
Mark left us. He had done his job and it was better he went
back. The Valcke brothers and Voss stayed with the bicycles.
The fewer people on the actual spot, the better.

Divoy went first through the hedge to open the doors and I
waited for his return. Somewhere a farm dog barked and I
wished it would shut up. It was quite dark now and very
quiet. Occasionally a branch stirred as a slight breeze found it
and rustled its leaves and once some small animal scurried
across the grass beside my feet.

What the hell was keeping Divoy? I strained my ears but
couldn't hear a sound. Then I heard movement ahead and
Divoy loomed up. Even in the dark I could see his face. He
looked in despair. He bent his mouth to my ear.

33

"They've changed the locks!" he whispered in a voice choking with rage, frustration and despair. "They've bloody-well-changed-the-God-damned-locks!"

5

Contact

I stared at Divoy in disbelief.

"They . . . they can't have . . ." I muttered, not wanting to believe that after we had come this far, so near, something had finally gone completely wrong.

"I tell you they have!"

We cursed together silently, letting out all our rage and frustration. Then another thought occurred to both of us at the same time. If the locks had been changed then there must be a reason. Had someone noticed something? Why? Why?

We decided to do something quick. The obvious thing was to go while the going was good, reluctant though we were to give up. But we could not take the petrol and the other heavy things. These we hid carefully nearby; and we returned to Stockel with me sitting on the cross-bar of Voss's bicycle.

Back home I could not sleep. All night I tossed and turned worrying over our plan and what might have gone wrong. I guessed that the lock change must have been done for some obscure German administrative reason and that they had not even bothered to look inside the shed. Otherwise surely they would have noticed something and been lying in wait for us? No, it was not that. It was just the sheer, dreadful let-down after hopes had been so high.

In the morning my family asked no questions. Now we had to start over again. Another visit to the shed, this time to get details of the new padlock. I began to scour every hardware shop in town and spent hours rummaging among the junk stalls on the 'Fleamarket'. No luck. I found padlocks of every shape and size except what we wanted. We could, of course, have used bolt croppers to cut the padlock but we wanted to use a key so as to postpone discovery of our flight as long as possible and so that we could push the aircraft back and maybe have a

35

chance to do it again if something were wrong at the last moment before starting-up. Finally I had an inspiration. I asked myself: had whoever was responsible for the change not gone to the local hardware shop near to Terbloc?

There I found a padlock similar to the one on the door. To my question "had some German bought a padlock of the same type?" the shop-keeper answered "yes, not long ago". I bought one which seem to me identical.

The next night I was at Terbloc again and again full of hope. Minor disaster! The key did not turn the lock but, as I soon discovered, only because of a small difference which we could easily put right ourselves. Much worse was when I went to check our petrol supply and found that this, together with the silencer, had vanished! We never found out how.

When I reported back, Divoy was in despair. Everything had gone so well and now everything was going wrong.

At least we could modify the key and pay one more visit to satisfy ourselves that our aircraft was still there. We thought of it as 'ours' by now, so familiar had we become with it. It was still there and apparently undisturbed. We locked up sadly and left, still pondering the fuel problem. Our Luftwaffe source of supply had dried up. The Feldwebel had been posted.

By one means or another I got in touch with certain escape organisations and began to think about this as an alternative. But to both Divoy and I it was now a point of pride to get out under our own steam; or rather on our own two wings. If only we had petrol!

Breyre in Liége thought he could help but would have big problems in getting the petrol through the various check points en route. Then Divoy had a tip from 'Miche' Jansen. Jansen was an ex-Air Force officer now working as an engineer at a gasworks near Brussels. Apparently Jansen could supply us with ordinary car petrol. Not only could Miche do this but he was ready to distil it for us to make it more suitable for use in the Stampe engine. On the 25th June we decided to make a thorough check of the engine and if possible start it. I was not so worried by the concealed bulk on the carrier of my bike as by the all-pervading smell of petrol which floated along with us and would surely have betrayed us at once if we had been stopped.

It was a good thing we made a thorough check. We discovered

a loose petrol union. Even if we had got going on the 19th this might have brought us to a sudden stop. So maybe Lady Luck was on our side after all. We tried for another oil sample and I muffed it, being slow to get the cap back on the drain vent. The result was a pool of oil on the cement floor under the engine. It took us an hour and all the rags we had, including Divoy's shirt, to get rid of this tell-tale mess. And we had to take the oil-soaked rags with us.

Then came the tricky part. We wanted to start the engine. Only one 'pop' would be sufficient but it would be a loud 'pop' in the quiet of the night and unfriendly ears were not far away. This was probably the most dangerous moment of the whole venture. Divoy was in the cockpit ready to switch off as soon as she fired. I turned the prop over by hand to suck in fuel. Once, twice, a third time. Ready? Contact!

One violent explosion shook the night before Divoy knocked the switch off. A thin film of light blue smoke came from the exhausts. It was enough. We knew she would go. It was also our signal to get the hell out of it fast. Even the dozing guards at the Chateau must have heard that bang and we wanted everything to be dark and quiet if they got around to investigating the shed. It was two in the morning, long after curfew and we cycled through the forest without lights, alert for any shadow ahead. That night I think we would have killed any wandering guard who tried to stop us. We seemed so near again.

Jansen had good news for us next day. He had managed to collect petrol and distil the twenty-odd gallons we needed. This had not been an easy job. Double the final quantity had to be obtained for distillation and this process was not completed without minor fires and breakages of equipment. Not only did Jansen have to get the petrol but also had to tell convincing stories to account for the fires and breakages and the use of the laboratory on Sundays. He took as big a risk as we did and for less reward. Later on we learned more about him. Such as, for instance, that he was an active member of the Resistance and was in touch with London by secret radio. Not only that but a message had actually been sent to London warning them of our expected arrival! This message, incidentally was hidden in the jacket of a courier who got caught en route between Jansen and the radio. So it was never sent but the courier hid the jacket and, in 1945, found it again with the message still hidden in the seam. However we were under the impression that it had got through and therefore we had to go soon. After all we did not want to keep Mr. Churchill waiting. He seemed a busy man.

We made this trip to Terbloc in style; in the back of the official 'Distrigaz' company car driven by Miche. Our faithful petrol carrier team were waiting for us at the edge of the forest and we quickly transferred the tins to their cycles. Then Miche left us since a car was an object of suspicion at any time; especially parked in a forest road. Divoy and I, the Valcke brothers and Robert Voss went quietly across the field trying to stop the tins clanking. Albert Valcke carried papers the Resistance had handed to him and which he would give to me at the last moment for 'airmail' delivery to London.

In the hangar we got ready. Divoy busied himself fitting the instrument panel whilst I stood on the wing and laboriously filled the fuel tank, a can at a time. The cans were heavy and by the time I had finished, my raincoat was soaked in petrol. It was 2.45 a.m. Time to get her out into the open.

Initially we had thought we could take-off straight from the hangar but we quickly realised not only would this mean pre-take-off noises very near to the Germans, but also that we might need the extra yards in which to get airborne. Everyone pushed, and we got the aircraft out of the hangar and back down to the far end of the field; not without many an anxious glance over our shoulders towards the Chateau; and many whispered exhortations to each other to keep it quiet.

The meadow was full of cows and Pierre Valcke was detailed off as temporary cowboy to run around, silently chase them into one bunch and keep them in the corner of the field out of the way.

At last there was nothing else left to be done. Divoy and I looked at each other and suddenly realised this was the big moment. We swallowed hard and solemnly shook hands with the others who had worked so hard and taken so many risks for us and whose only reward would be to see us disappear into the darkness headed for freedom.

I climbed into the front cockpit. All correct. Switches off. "Right. Suck in."

A swing of the propeller to draw in fuel. Then magneto switches on.

"Contact."

Divoy gave a mighty heave on the propeller blade and swung it round half a revolution. The engine coughed once. Another swing. A second cough followed by silence. A third and still no luck. Divoy and I changed places. I swung that propeller until the sweat poured off me but still the engine refused to start. By great good luck a stream of RAF bombers was passing overhead and I can only think that the noise of their engines distracted the Germans from hearing the clanks and coughs as we vainly tried to start that engine.

My watch said 3.30 a.m. Bitter pill though it was to swallow we had to face up to the fact that it was now too late to go. Furthermore the first fingers of dawn were paling the sky and, if we hung around much longer, detection was certain.

Sick at heart we pushed the Stampe back in the hangar. No one said anything. Divoy quietly began to take out the instrument panel. We had to leave everything just as if we had never been there. We did it like automatons, too dispirited to talk.

Divoy and I were both exhausted with prop swinging and so the Valcke brothers cycled back to town and we arranged that they should ask Miche Jansen to pick us up in his car at a quiet spot in the forest. He came at dawn, and found Divoy and myself fast asleep behind trees, surrounded by empty petrol tins, suitcases, revolvers, flying instruments and envelopes marked 'London. Secret' on the outside. What he had to say to us regarding our lack of security made our ears tingle but I suppose we deserved it. Frankly we were past caring after the awful let down of the last few hours.

By now my family had accepted my tearful farewells and sudden reappearances the next morning with resignation and without comment.

Two nights later we were back again. This time Miche Jansen had got something else for us, or rather someone else. Pierre Nottet was an aircraft engineer as well as an air force pilot and he had volunteered to try and find out why the Stampe engine would not start.

Divoy, Nottet and Miche worked in the hangar whilst I kept watch outside. So accustomed had we become to carrying on our clandestine activities that at first I couldn't believe it when I detected footsteps in the distance coming from the Chateau. I hissed a hurried warning to the others and they slipped out. I just had time to close the doors before joining them in a thick patch of bushes nearby. The unknown walker came nearer. He was whistling softly to himself. I remember it was the 'Radetzky March' and he was a bit out of key. As he came nearer I tightened my hand round the butt of my revolver and beside me Divoy had a spanner ready. The man, whoever he was, walked steadily on and we heard his footsteps pass into the forest and his whistle float away into the darkness. He never knew how near death he was at that moment.

Half-an-hour later the mystery of the engine was solved. The Stampe had been fitted with special throttles for inverted flying and we had inadvertently connected up the linkage the wrong way so that when we thought the throttle was open it was in fact shut!

It was again too late to do anything that night. We tidied up and covered our traces and melted back into the forest and headed home. This time we set a date and it was to be the following Friday, the 4th July. Someone reminded me it was American Independence Day and I thought it was as good a date as any.

Jansen persuaded us to change our usual routine. We should have done it long ago, but hadn't thought about it in our eagerness to get things ready.

Divoy and I were to meet up and go together to Jansen's house. He would then drive us out in his car and leave it in the garden of a friend's house for his return journey.

Once again we counted the hours and felt the tension build up and our stomachs get tighter. So often had we made the trip out to Terbloc and so often had our hopes been dashed at the last minute. Just what could go wrong next? We couldn't think of anything but no doubt Lady Luck would still have a nasty one up her sleeve!

There were only two people on the rear platform of the tram out to Miche's home. Myself and a German S.S. officer. All the way, he never took his eyes off me and carefully inspected every inch, taking in my raincoat, my red scarf and my boots. I hoped his eyes were not too penetrating for in my grip were the revolvers and under the raincoat I was in uniform.

I decided to take the initiative and smiled at him. Unexpectedly under his peaked cap his face broke into an answer-

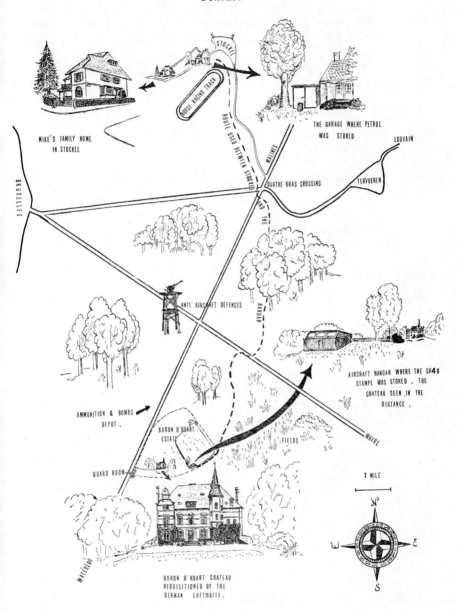

Sketch map illustrating the highlights of the escape route from the author's family home on the outskirts of Brussels to the take-off point. (Map drawn by the author's son)

41

ing tight-lipped smile and he moved off inside the tram and sat down. I got off at the next stop just to get out of the way of those eyes.

It was a lovely evening with the sort of sunset which promises a fine night and a day to follow. As planned Divoy, Miche and I got out to Groenendael in Jansen's car. To wait for darkness we sat on the terrace of the village café and drank a beer or two, chatting with forced nonchalance about anything we could think of to take our minds off what might lie ahead.

Following our usual route down the lane and through the trees we quickly opened the shed after fixing the instruments. Jansen and Divoy embarked on the last check of the aircraft and then we sat and waited until the exact time we had planned came round. That was the worst. The waiting, with the meadow in bright moonlight and the lights from the Chateau. The windows were obviously open and we could hear voices louder than usual.

Two a.m. We got to our feet and, pushing and grunting, got the Stampe moving across the grass. We could still see the wheel marks left when we had pushed her out last. Why in God's name had no one else noticed them?

We got her down to the end of the field. Then it was hand-shakes again and Divoy and I climbed up to the cockpit.

Jansen handed up to us the papers we had to take to London and I stowed them away securely. We had wrapped them in a petrol-soaked rug so we could destroy them easily if necessary.

The hands of Divoy's beloved alarm clock on the instrument panel ticked off the last few minutes to 2.45 a.m. This was it!

"Ready?'

"All set."

"Switches off."

"Switches off. Suck-in."

A couple of turns of the propeller.

"Contact?"

"Contact."

Jansen took a firm grip on the propeller blade, heaved it over compression, then skipped quickly back.

The motor coughed, spluttered, fired and then Divoy had it caught on the throttle and it broke into an ear-splitting roar! The night's silence was shattered. Jansen ran round to the side of the cockpit and punched each of our arms in turn.

"Bon voyage!" he yelled above the engine. No need to whisper now. We knew that if the Germans came running it would take them five minutes to reach us but the engine had to warm up. I saw Jansen by now running away into the shadows and I was half out of my seat with impatience for Divoy to get that throttle open. We held it for two minutes, then the fuselage vibrated as the throttle went wide and the engine took on a louder roar. Slowly we began to trundle forward over the grass, then faster and faster. The Stampe bounced along and I felt the tail lift. Bounce, thud, bounce, another thud. The black shadowy trees were beginning to blur past now and I thought I could hear shouting. I had my revolver cocked and ready over the side. Nothing, no one was going to stop us now! I felt the control column ease back. She rose, sank again then came up and suddenly the jolting had ceased and we were airborne!

Then the stick jolted forward and we pitched down into a dive heading straight for the trees. We both had our hands on the control column. I was in front and Divoy with the dual control was in the rear cockpit. We pulled hard and she came up, wheels and wings brushing the leaves. Then we were up and over the trees. I saw the ground drop away and the forest and Terbloc and the shed and the field fall into the dark behind. Up, up through the night sky we climbed, the little engine roaring away as if it, too, was joyous at being in the air again. At 10,000 feet Divoy levelled off. I don't know what he felt like but my mind was a whirl of excitement, relief, and sheer unmitigated surprise that we seemed to have done it. I twisted round and I could see his face split in a triumphant grin. He reached one arm forward over the cowling between the two cockpits. I reached mine back and we grasped hands. I leaned my head back, looked up at the stars and laughed outright.

I checked our course as best I could. About sixty degrees left of the Pole Star would give us a true course of about three-zero-zero degrees and this would bring us to England. The little engine sang sweetly. Now it was everything to us. All our hopes and our future, in this world or the next, hung on that engine.

We could make out Ghent and the Scheldt estuary. This meant we had drifted too far north and had to correct. Divoy banked to port until we thought it was about right, then levelled off again. Suddenly we both shot bolt upright as the aircraft, us and the sky were bathed in a sudden white glare. Then we

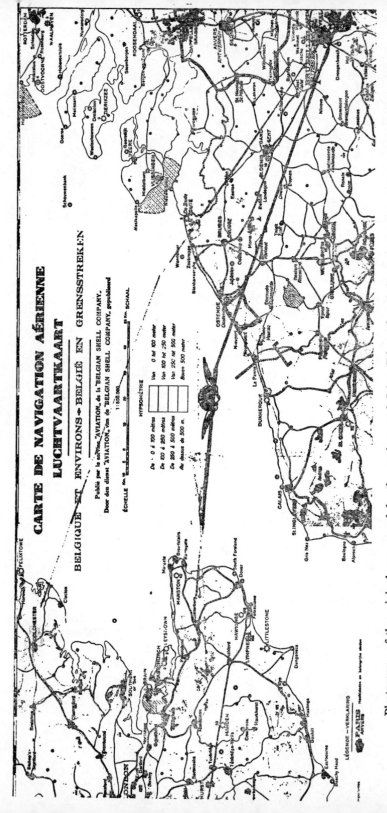

Photo-copy of the original map used by the author and Léon Divoy for their escape flight from Brussels. The southerly track is the planned flight path, the northerly one is that actually followed. The original of this chart is in the Musée de l'Armée in Brussels.

realised it was a searchlight groping for us across the sky. It missed us and the beam swept on leaving us in the dark as we crossed the coast and saw the dull, silver glimmer of the sea.

Then the motor died away! All at once silence, emptiness and despair. We madly jerked throttles, switched on and off, turned fuel-cocks every way. Nothing happened. We continued gliding silently through the night: the sea which now looked cold and hostile, waiting for us below. Suddenly I remembered we had forgotten to bring the two old car inner tubes which were to be our survival gear. "I can't swim," came Divoy's voice over the headphones. He sounded gloomy. I didn't know if he were joking or not. By now it was too late to consider a forced landing inland or on a beach. We were down to a thousand feet and bracing ourselves for a wet, crash landing.

Then, as suddenly as it had stopped, the engine picked up! The unbelievable had happened. Why or how we never knew but there were all the pistons pumping up and down again like mad and all the valves popping open and shut and that blessed roar of power once again.

Slowly we regained altitude and with every revolution of the propeller our escape grew more certain. Even if that engine did it again on us surely we could now glide down to somewhere where a British ship or aircraft would see us.

As we cruised along under the stars I wondered about that engine. What had caused it to stop at that crucial moment and why was it running rough now and cutting intermittently? Luck had been on our side, as when the engine cut first the sudden silence must have put off the anti-aircraft sound detectors which were used by the Germans to bring the guns to bear and start shooting. Then when it picked up low this might have been a trick of Lady Luck. If at all she would keep her keen "supervision" of our flight a little longer. This was my prayer.

Divoy had a splendid sense of occasion and it did not fail him on this one. He groped around in his cockpit and reached his arm forward to me again. This time, it was a bottle of brandy and together under the stars, at several thousand feet and half-way to England, we drank our toast to freedom!

Nevertheless we were not out of trouble even yet. Every time we reached 3,000 feet the motor started to cough and splutter. It began to feel very cold. Just before sunrise I took over the controls and behind me the blackness of the sky began to pale as a hint of the coming dawn. Ahead and above the stars continued to glitter. It seemed as if a million eyes were watching us with amused interest; just to see if we would make it, or plunge into the grey sea stretching from horizon to horizon.

I realised all at once that the horizon ahead was broken slightly here and there from its level line. It must be the English coast. Nearer and nearer came the faint line where sky and sea joined and then suddenly it was a line no longer but the loom of a flat, muddy coast pierced with watery inlets. I pored over the map but could find nothing resembling what I saw below. I could now make out sandbanks and mud flats with flocks of gulls roosting at the end of their night's sleep. At this moment the rim of the sun slid above the horizon behind us and all at once it was green fields below. I made out a road and a farmhouse or two. If only the coast defences let us alone, we had it made! Come to think of it, where were those defences? We had thought to find the English coast bristling and alert and that we would certainly be intercepted by fighters. It seemed almost an insult to have come in an hour or two from enemy-occupied Europe and to be greeted with such sleepy, morning indifference.

This quiet had me worried. Had something gone wrong with our navigation? Had we unknowingly in the dark gone round in a circle. Was the land below not a welcoming England but a very inhospitable Holland or France?

The engine began spluttering again and we realised that we would have to make a landing somewhere; preferably in a spot of our own choosing while we still had some power. In any event we had only about fifteen minutes' fuel left so the matter was really beyond any decision we might make.

We peered over the side, Divoy to port and I to starboard. Then I called Divoy to my side and he saw exactly what we had been looking for. A nice, level-looking field between a road and a railway line. We flew round it in approved, initial flying school manner, inspecting the surface. It looked O.K. Divoy continued round across the downwind end of the field, flew back up then turned in, sideslipping to lose height. He straightened out, cut the motor, and eased the stick back. There was a gentle shiver, a bump, then another bump and we were down. We rolled jerkily a few yards then slowed to a stop. The engine cut

46

and we sat there in silence. Somewhere a bird commenced his morning song and a little wind rippled the grass of the field.

"Good man," I said to Divoy. "Another landing like that and you'll be fit for solo."

We still were not sure if we had made it. It might not be England.

We scrambled stiffly from the machine. Over to one side there was a small wood, ideally placed to hide fugitive aviators not sure which country they are in. We made a bee-line for it and hid our belongings. Then we took a careful look around.

At one end of the field we saw something we had not noticed before. It was a farm-house with a red tiled roof. Obviously that should be our first port of call. Stepping cautiously across the grass we could see a farm cart standing in the yard. It had something on the side. "Smith Brothers & Sons." Divoy read it slowly. "Sounds English enough," he said. I nodded. We pushed open the gate. Then I nudged Divoy. "This is England all right."

"How can you tell?"

I chuckled.

"Look at those bedroom windows. Open. Only the English sleep with their windows open all night!"

As for the English people, their first representative came round the corner at that moment. He was an oldish man with a white moustache. I summoned up my best English. "Good morning. Please, where is this place?"

He looked startled and replied automatically, never taking his eyes off us.

"Thorpe-le-Soken."

"Is that in England?"

He seemed astonished at such a question.

" 'Course it is. In Essex."

6

To War Again

The next minute he was backing anxiously away from two excited, laughing, mad foreigners, trying to embrace him and pump his hand. He was still staring after us, shaking his head in amazement, as we wandered off up the lane in search of the nearest police station.

The second Englishman we met was on a bicycle and we stopped him and asked the way to the police station. He offered to show us and fell in step, pushing his cycle. Divoy tried to tell him something about where we had come from. Either he did not believe us or else was just showing the traditional English politeness towards mad foreigners. His conversation seemed to consist entirely of "Well I'll be blowed", or "Get away! Is that so?"

After all we had been through, events at the police station were pure farce. We met one policeman in uniform standing in front of the open door. We carefully explained we were Belgian airmen who had stolen an aeroplane from occupied Europe and flown it here and please could we report to someone? He listened in polite silence then smiled grimly at us.

"And whose leg do you think you're pulling?" he asked bluntly. Divoy pulled out his wallet and waved an identity card under the constable's nose. Then we heard footsteps on the stairs and another policeman, sleepy-eyed and tousled, came in tying the loop of a dressing gown.

"What the devil's happening here," he said. "I'm the sergeant-in-charge."

The first policeman jerked a thumb at us.

"These two jokers are trying to tell me they've just landed from Belgium or somewhere. Say they took an aircraft from the other side."

The Sergeant rubbed his chin. It was bristly at that hour. "Can you prove it?"

I thought of the most convincing proof there was and told him where he would find not only the aircraft but all our gear stowed away in the wood.

"Right," he said. "You," pointing at Divoy, "You go and show the constable." To me he added "You stay here."

While he went on to shave and to get dressed, the first constable left with Divoy while I stayed with a second policeman who had come out from the station. Half an hour later Divoy and his escort were back laden with luggage and bits and pieces from the aircraft. Obviously the constable was now thoroughly convinced and he and Divoy were on the best of terms.

The constable addressed himself to the Sergeant.

"Do you know. They've actually done it. They've actually been and gone and pinched a ruddy aeroplane from right under Jerry's nose and got here with it. Last night. You know they're never going to believe this one higher up."

The sergeant got busy on the telephone, still chuckling, and obviously enjoying having to make this somewhat unusual report.

By now the sergeant's wife had come in and been told all about it. Fifteen minutes later we were being ushered in to a monumental breakfast. Bacon, eggs, lovely white bread and pots and pots of steaming English tea. We sat there, just soaking up the peace and winding down after all the tension of the last few weeks. It was heavenly.

An hour later the first of what became a stream of visitors, representing a dozen different interested authorities began to arrive. To each the story had to be told. Some were interested; others downright suspicious whilst others were there just to make sure we filled in the necessary forms. There was even an Immigration officer and we had him really worried. Apparently in war-time England arrival could only take place at certain defined points and Thorpe-le-Soken was not one of them. Finally, in despair, he asked us to agree Harwich as our point of arrival; this being the nearest approved port of entry. Europe might be under the tyrant's heel; the British Empire in mortal peril; but the form had to be filled-in just the same!

The local Army commander was most disgruntled that we had entered England so easily and obviously considered it our fault entirely that he would have some explaining to do. As for the Air Force people who came along later they had eyes only for our Stampe and insisted on our explaining to them every detail of the work we had done. Someone suggested our instrument panel (including Divoy's alarm clock) might end up in the British Museum! Anyway they promised us they would look after everything carefully for us.

Later things became much more official and formal. We were interrogated about every detail of our lives over the past twenty-four hours. We had to turn out all our pockets whilst a list was made of everything we had. This included, in my case, eight figs I had brought. During the compiling of the list I ate one.

"Funny," said the official, "I could have sworn there were eight."

He carefully altered the figures on the form. Then I ate another, and another and each time he amended the quantity entered on the form. By the time we came to the end I had to point out to him that he might as well delete the word 'figs' altogether since there were none left. I had eaten them all.

Quite a crowd gathered to see us off. We shook hands with the sergeant, the constable and the sergeant's wife. Then we got into the car and took our first journey through the English countryside. We drove to a railway station and caught an afternoon train to London. Don't ask me my first impressions of England on that journey. As soon as we had settled down I fell asleep until we reached London.

London! The magic name! Rows and rows of roof-tops and chimney pots from horizon to horizon. Miles of neat surburban houses looking all alike; parks with camouflaged anti-aircraft guns in them; fat barrage balloons swaying indolently in the sky at the end of their slender cables. This was the capital of the free world, the voice and hope towards which millions in enslavement were looking.

We left the train at the big terminal of Liverpool Street and took a taxi, all four of us. Our escort gave the driver an address but it meant nothing to Divoy and me. We drove on through seemingly endless streets and finally, in a quiet residential road, pulled up before a building which reminded me of nothing so much as a convent. But this convent had a sentry at the door and barbed wire round it.

It seemed to be some sort of military mess or hostel. We were past caring about details like that. Less than twenty-four hours before we had been in the cockpit at Terbloc waiting to take off. Now we were tucked up in comfortable beds somewhere in the middle of London! It was just too awe-inspiring to worry about so we fell asleep.

"Do you realise that we would have been shot, had we been caught?" These were the words by which Divoy woke me up next morning after our first London night. I had vaguely thought of this and of the risk I was taking. I did not imagine we could fail so maybe I was helping Lady Luck along.

The first forty-eight hours of our stay in England were spent answering questions. We had to remember all we could about German defences and troops in Belgium; what the food ration was like; what people thought about things; morale and a hundred-and-one other questions until we were hoarse with talking.

Later we were given some English money and allowed to join others like us in the canteen. There were French sailors, Senegalese and escapers from every country in Europe. There was even another Belgian Air Force pilot, Michael de Hepcée. We were a bit proud of our own escape story but here it was just one more; and some of them were really hair-curling. The main topic for everyone seemed to be speculation as to how soon they could get back into uniform and in what branch of the Service. Someone asked Divoy and I if we would be willing to be parachuted back into Belgium. After all the trouble we had gone to simply to get out we thought it rather a pointless question! We gently pointed out that the whole object of the exercise had been to fight on in the air.

An order came for us to report to the office of the Belgian Air Attaché in Town. We went there by taxi. London was alive with people. We saw some bomb damage but nothing like the German propaganda had made out. At the Embassy in Eaton Square we found we had no money to pay the taxi. We asked one of the two Gendarmes at the entrance to pay for us but he rather hurriedly declined, obviously mistrusting our appearance. Someone lent us the cab fare and we paid off the patient driver.

Getting up the stairs we met Colonel Wouters, the attaché, just emerging from his office.

"Good morning sir," we chorused, giving him a smart salute.

He scrutinised us carefully.

"And who might you two be?"

We told him.

51

"And when did you arrive in England?"

"Early Saturday morning, sir."

"And when did you leave Belgium?"

"Precisely two hours and thirty minutes before, sir."

He inspected us even closer.

"Good God! I think you had better come in and tell me about it."

In the Colonel's office we once again went over our story. At the end of it the Colonel invited us to lunch at the Royal Automobile Club and there we met Commandant Cajot, an old acquaintance from Bierset and, incidentally, a 1914–1918 veteran. He had arrived in England in 1940 leading a group of trainees from the flying school there.

Over lunch we heard news of former friends. We heard of those who had gone straight into the Battle of Britain, some of whom had been killed. Ortmans had been shot down twice; Offenberg had four confirmed 'kills' and had been awarded the British Distinguished Flying Cross. Many other names were mentioned.

By this time the Belgian colony in London had heard about us and we had to call on all kinds of people in exile and each time tell our story again and again. We enjoyed London. Even the air smelt different. After all, it *was* different. It was free.

Jan Offenberg, by then a flight commander in 609 Squadron at Biggin Hill, came up especially to see us. He too had escaped from France in a small Caudron Simoun machine just before the collapse, and brought Jottard with him in the second seat. I had seen Offenberg's father and mother just before we left and was able to give him all the latest family news.

Then we had a real thrill. They laid on for us a visit to 609 squadron and suddenly we were back in the atmosphere of a fighter squadron. We drooled over the sleek Spitfires and wondered how long it would be before we could get our hands on one. Meanwhile the press had a field-day with us, both British and American, and we recorded several interviews for radio broadcasts. We were also promoted. Although arrived as sergeant cadet-officers, we were commissioned as Second Lieutenants from then on. I must admit on reflection that it was the hardest promotion I ever earned!

July 21st was a great day for us. A parade was held at Wellington Barracks where the re-constituted Belgian Land

Forces paraded for the first time as a whole. Several Air Force officers were decorated by the Prime Minister and I must admit to a strong emotion when I heard the "Brabançonne" played in public for the first time since the 10th May, 1940.

Meanwhile what had happened back in Belgium after we left? Of course it was a long time later before I learned the full details. My brother Mark knew everything that had been going on and when he returned home the evening after we left and realised I wasn't there he knew something must have happened.

He first tried to contact Voss and the Valcke brothers. All three were temporarily absent, no doubt prudently lying low for a few days until any fuss had died down. Eventually he managed to contact Voss but even he knew nothing. Apparently on the last night, Voss had arrived home too late for him to be able to answer my request for help.

Later he made contact with Jansen who told him all about the successful take-off. Jansen had watched us career across the field and caught his breath as we made that dive towards the trees and just cleared them. A friend of Jansen had been briefed to listen to the sky on the other side of Brussels and had reported hearing our engine going strong and dying away to the west.

Beyond that they could find out nothing and simply had to continue listening to the BBC for a coded message of some kind. There was nothing on the Sunday evening broadcast but on Monday the Belgian Defence Minister, speaking from London, mentioned something about the success of Belgian fighter pilots with the RAF and then went on to talk about two German pilots who had arrived recently in a small aircraft. This seemed a most odd story and they wondered if it was a hint of some kind. Not until Saturday could Miche Jansen come up with anything positive. He told the others he had good reason to believe we had made it but it wasn't as yet one hundred-per-cent confirmed.

By then the Germans put a million-franc fine on the village of Overyse, in whose bounds Terbloc lies, unless they produced information about Thierry d'Huart and his aircraft. Apparently Thierry could not be found either. It was said that the German personnel working in the Chateau were all court-martialled and given military jail sentences. Later Thierry d'Huart was located. He was still in Belgium and managed to convince the Germans he knew nothing whatever about the disappearance of his aircraft.

Monday 14th July, the BBC broadcast something which immediately told everyone "in-the-know" about our safe arrival. Apparently there was quite a little celebration. The message simply said that:— "A corporal of the third sends kisses to all his family from TVBABBBC". Divoy's nickname was Caporal and he was in 3 Squadron; whilst my nickname was Bonne Balle. So that signature was an abbreviation for 'Tout va bien á bord, Bonne Balle, Caporal.'

Later one of my uncles visited the family and related with some pride a story he had heard on the BBC about two Belgian pilots having escaped. My family dare not tell him it was his own nephew. The fewer people who knew the better; for them and everyone else.

As far as events at Terbloc went, a local farmer, who owned the cows we had herded, went to the field next morning and found the hangar doors open. He looked at the tyre marks on the wet grass and drew his own conclusions. He deemed it prudent to wait a few hours before reporting to the estate manager. This worthy also 'forgot' to mention it to the Germans until he had, as he thought, given whoever was up to whatever it was, another few hours to get away with it. Occupation by an enemy might not be very pleasant but it sharpened up wits wonderfully!

The Germans were flabbergasted when they found the hangar empty. It seemed that shortly before we left they had decided to take the aircraft to Evère to use as a trainer and had changed the locks only to prevent anyone who might get wind of their intentions from getting in and doing damage. They had no idea that the 'damage' had already begun some time before. Sentries were interrogated and said they had heard an aircraft engine but thought a British aircraft was attacking at low level and they had promptly dived for cover! The estate bailiff and the farmer were also interrogated but were finally cleared of complicity.

Thierry d'Huart managed to establish his innocence, as has been mentioned, but only by producing the original instrument panel from the aircraft. Later it transpired that the guards at the Chateau had not received prison terms but something which most Germans considered much worse . . . a posting to the

Russian front! On the other side of the coin we learned much later that a group of Luftwaffe pilots at a Mess in Brussels had laughed loud and long when they heard of our exploit and said the German equivalent of 'Best of luck to 'em!'

Back to events in England, we paid a visit to an airfield near London to say farewell to 'our' little Stampe. It looked so small in the huge hangar. For so many months it had been the centre of our lives and everything had revolved around it. It had done its job nobly and well and we felt quite sad at parting from it.

Then the summons we had been waiting for came from the Air Ministry: to report to an Operational Training Unit in Scotland for refresher training. However we had done some quiet homework and discovered beforehand that a similar course was about to start at Heston, just outside London. By cajolery and persuasion we managed to get our posting changed to Heston. Other Belgian pilots whom we knew already had also been assigned to this course. Also at Heston we would convert to the Spitfire whereas Scotland meant Hurricanes. Not that there was anything wrong with the Hurricane. It was simply that the Spitfire was the aircraft which had caught all our imaginations and was faster. Not until later did we learn of the great work the Hurricane had done in the Battle of Britain and the advantages of its rugged, simple construction which allowed it to take terrific punishment and still keep on flying.

The next day we passed our medical check. This had worried us a little since we did not know to what extent our reduced diet back home had effected our fitness. Anyway we were O.K. Perhaps it was all that bicycling to and from Terbloc! We were also commissioned again, this time as Pilot Officers of the Royal Air Force. The tailor rose to the challenge and in a couple of days we were strolling down Piccadilly as a couple of brand-new 'sprog' pilot officers with bright new RAF wings which we had won without ever setting foot in an RAF cockpit.

The same evening in a Richmond pub I met a group of the Home Guard, civilian spare-time volunteers. One of them slid a .303 round from his rifle magazine and asked me to put it into the ammunition belt of my aircraft so that he could get in a crack at the enemy.

By now we were in a daze, things moving so quickly. However Heston was to bring us smartly down to earth again. There was a very operational feeling about the station, the instructors being all ex-Battle of Britain veterans handing on their experience to us. Now it had got so far, both Divoy and I were beginning to have qualms. After all there was quite a difference between a Spitfire and the Renard which was the last machine I had piloted in combat; or the Fairey Fox which Divoy had been handling.

The pupils on the course were an odd mixture of nationalities. Two of these were French pilots who had escaped to Gibraltar in a French Air Force Martin Maryland bomber. They had evaded both their own and German fighters before running the gauntlet of the Gibraltar defences. My instructor was Sergeant Whip, who seemed a likeable enough chap. Our first flights were on the Miles Master trainer just to get the feel of an aircraft again. The approaches to Heston were not easy, with residential streets close to the boundary and on my first flight with Whip I incurred his displeasure by some pretty hectic handling of the controls. I was not just wanting to show off; it was the sheer delight of holding a joy-stick again. I did not know then about the RAF's very high and very strict standards of flying discipline.

I felt hurt and slighted when the deputy flight commander recommended more dual for me before I could go solo. Divoy and others had gone solo so why not me? I thought he was too cautious and 'stick-in-the-mud'. Major Guillaume, the senior Belgian officer, an experienced instructor, realised that there were personality problems involved and personally checked me out. With him I felt quite relaxed and a couple of flights later they sent me off solo.

On 5th August I soloed in a Spitfire!

I felt like a young man on his first date. I climbed up to the cockpit and the mechanic helped me with the straps. Then I taxied carefully out across the grass, peering anxiously each side of the long nose poking out and up beyond the windscreen. I did not want to damage this beautiful thing on the ground.

Turning into the wind I went over everything in my mind. All O.K. I pushed open the throttle and felt the airframe vibrate with the sheer power of the roaring Merlin engine. We shot across the grass like a catapult and I remembered to be alert for, and to check, the swing to the left they had warned me about. Then we were off the ground. Wheels up, everything normal and zooming up into the clear blue sky. It was magnificent! I felt intoxicated with the joy of flying. Never, never had there been so perfect a flying machine as this. She was powerful, strong, yet light as a feather and responded to every touch of the controls. I climbed, dived, did steep turns, climbed again. Soon my flying time was up and I slid down into a left-hand circuit, turned cross-wind, throttled back and sank down to earth like a drifting leaf. Marvellous!

Every day we could see the Polish squadron, from nearby Northolt, take-off for sweeps over France. Their broken-up formations on return was some evidence of the air fighting which had taken place. Another day I had to land at Gravesend and I did so just in time to watch 609 Squadron return from a sortie. The pilots looked tired and strained, I listened to their descriptions of combat: and expressive hand gestures to describe the dog-fight manoeuvres all over the sky. Beside them I felt like a raw recruit which, to some extent, I was.

At the end of August our introduction to a modern fighting aircraft finished, but we still had much to learn. Whilst waiting for a posting, Divoy and I took the opportunity to go and see our old friend, the little Stampe. By now she, too, had acquired a new uniform being re-painted in RAF camouflage colours. She also had a brand new registration number J 7777. We had some influence in allocation of this number. The letter 'J' stood for a girl friend of mine whose name was Joan; whilst the '7777' was a hint that both Divoy and I had been on No. 77 Course at Flying Training School in Belgium. We were allowed to fly her once again and had a glorious half hour of aerobatics over Heston.

Our postings came through . . . to 64 Squadron at Turnhouse in Scotland. This did not appeal to us very much. It seemed a long way from the action. However we had to accept that, with only thirty odd flying hours to our credit and not as yet fully fit after privations in Belgium, perhaps it was a good thing.

Our new station was near Edinburgh and there we met our CO, Squadron-Leader Barry Heath. Among the pilots I was happily surprised to meet an ex-observer I had known at Bierset, Charles Mertens, and another Belgian, 'Moustique' Gonay who had been my former flying instructor.

There was not much action at Turnhouse. Daily patrols over the Firth of Forth and the naval base at Rosyth, together with cover over assembling or returning convoys. There was the occasional scramble against intruders having a go at coastal shipping but not much else. We later found out about the terrific hammering 64 Squadron had taken over Dunkirk and during the Battle of Britain and realised that this spell up north was more in the way of a rest and a re-fit. Thus we stood a chance of moving south again before long.

We soon made good friends among the RAF members of the Squadron. We were introduced to squadron history and legend; picked up the RAF slang and soon got the party spirit of gathering round the beer-soaked mess piano and singing traditional, if unprintable, songs. We were shown the mysteries of the operations control room where the movement of every aircraft were plotted minute-by-minute on a large map with information derived by a magic thing called radar. This was a real eye-opener for us. Neither Belgium nor any other country had anything like this in our experience.

Our Spitfires were the Mark II version having an up-rated Merlin engine and a cartridge engine starter. On my first flight over the Firth I detected quite a bit more power available at my finger tips.

Divoy and I had both been put into 'B' Flight and every day we learned more about combat flying. We practised dog fighting, formation flying and cloud and instrument flying. My first effort at formation flying was not an outstanding success and I seemed to be forever throttling back to avoid shooting ahead and immediately having to put the throttle forward again so as not to get left behind. However we improved with practice. We had to learn operational procedures and how to follow instructions from a ground controller. In dog-fighting I was 'shot down' many times by my instructors. Several times I 'blacked-out' pulling so very tight a turn but it always seemed as if my opponent was on my tail again in a couple of turns. Fortunately all he was aiming at me was a camera gun and afterwards we could go over the film together and see just what I had done wrong and what I ought to have done at that moment. "You're not just learning to fight. You're learning to survive in order to fight," they told me. I could see their point.

We had a change one day when, with another officer, I was detailed to sail aboard a destroyer tasked with escorting a convoy down the East Coast. I was none too keen since it seemed to me a waste of valuable flying time, but I had to go.

58

Soon after departure the ship's officers were able to prove to me that it was no pleasure cruise. The convoy consisted of fifty merchant vessels and the sea was sown with mines and no doubt populated by U-Boats out for some juicy hunting. That night I wondered how the ships ever kept together or how the escort kept so close to them. It was pitch black and all one could see were the outline of one's companion on the bridge, the stars overhead and a feather of bow wave from the forward part of the hull.

Next morning I woke to a thick blanket of fog and the difficult job the sailors were doing came home to me yet again. About noon, a rising wind dispelled the fog and an hour or two later we heard a thud as a torpedo struck a ship on the far side from us. The convoy could not stop and as night fell we could still see her burning, back on the horizon.

We duly delivered our convoy to the Thames and almost immediately turned back to escort another one northwards. As night fell we suddenly saw flashes in the sky ahead and distant thumps. The radio crackled that a pack of E-Boats had found, and were attacking the convoy. We had expected something like it for in the afternoon a German reconnaissance machine had done a couple of orbits far above. The main attack was some way from us but we could hear the crackle of gun-fire and the steady thump-thump of the naval automatic guns. Then it was our turn to open up and one hell of a din broke loose all round me. Between bangs, flashes and seeing tracer shells curving away across the sea I could not figure out what they were firing at. However when things quietened down we heard that our ship was being officially credited with one E-boat damaged whilst another was sunk by a sister-ship up ahead.

Nothing else happened until the following night when we were just off Newcastle-on-Tyne and in time to watch a German air raid on that city. We could see the flash of explosions, hear the crump of anti-aircraft and watch the shells bursting in the sky mingled with flares drifting down. Three times I saw tracer flash across the sky high above as a night-fighter closed in behind a raider and each time I watched a ball of fire suddenly blossom and fall slowly down to earth as the target was hit.

We arrived back at Turnhouse with a healthy respect for the Navy's activities and an even healthier one for the crews of the merchant ships.

The next day I was briefed for a dusk flying exercise as a preliminary to night flying at a later stage. The weather was cloudy but visibility fair. I had a little trouble on my first two landings. The Turnhouse runways were somewhat short for a Spitfire but I made two reasonable efforts. I took-off again for my third 'circuit-and-bump' but this time I was obstructed on the approach by another aircraft and had to open up and go round again. On my next try yet another aircraft, this time a Blenheim, got in my way and again I had to overshoot and spend five minutes orbiting at height before flying control called me in. By this time darkness had set in and it was no longer a dusk landing but a real night attempt. I was a bit tired and very frustrated. Control finally gave the word and I set up an approach for the third time. Pitch fully fine . . . flaps down. Under my helmet I was sweating a little. Then damn it! Another red light. Full power, flaps up and round we went yet again, the Spitfire and I.

Coming in this time I was concentrating on getting the flare path lined up just right and although it annoyed me I had no time to wonder what that funny horn noise was, blaring away in the cockpit. I throttled back, flared out and again wondered why the hell they were flashing a red light from behind me! In that instant, as the Spitfire sank to the ground, a horrible grating noise came through from outside and I saw sparks flying. I had landed wheels-up!

The aircraft slid for about a hundred yards then came to rest lop-sidedly. The fire tender and crash wagon were racing out but I didn't need them. What I really needed was a nice, large hole in the ground in which to bury myself, so ashamed did I feel.

Apparently on overshooting after my last abortive approach I still had 'wheels down' selected. On the final approach, so accustomed had I become to following a set pattern that I automatically reached for the undercarriage operating knob without realising that I would actually be pulling the wheels up instead of putting them down. It cost me a few drinks in the Mess to live that one down!

What upset me rather more was the feeling that, having dropped a stupid 'clanger' like this, from there on I was being watched very carefully and could not afford the slightest mistake in future.

We had a squadron deployment, not far away. To Drem, near the mouth of the Firth for some more interminable convoy protection duty. Apart from thinking that the Scottish coastline and scenery were really very beautiful from the air there was little to do on these flights except accumulate flying hours.

Then came the news that the squadron was posted south! We were due to relieve 611 Squadron at Hornchurch, near London. What's more we would leave behind us our Spitfire II's and at Hornchurch would have the much more up-to-date Spitfire 5's.

Next day we left for the real shooting war.

7

Wing Formation

Hornchurch was similar to most of the other RAF airfields I had seen. Three large hangars and brick-built administrative buildings and technical sections. Here and there gaps and the odd bit of rubble showed some of the pounding it had received during the Battle of Britain. It had been established during the First World War as a base for squadrons protecting London. One of that squadron's pilots had shot down an airship and a piece of its structure was mounted and occupied a prominent place in the Mess.

At that time the Hornchurch wing consisted of ourselves plus 603 Squadron; whilst a third, 411 Canadian Squadron was due a few days after us. Of these only 603 had recent operational experience. The Wing Commander in charge of flying and wing leader was Eric Stapleton.

He welcomed us and told us over a drink that now we were down for some real business. The Station Commander, Harry Broadhurst, was away in the United States. He was leading a team of the top fighter pilots who had gone over to lecture over their experiences in air fighting during the last two years. Harry Broadhurst was one of the toughest fighter and the best leaders in the air of 11 Group.

He was known in pre-war days for leading the formation aerobatic at the Hendon display. In air combat he had made fame by his aggressiveness and his shooting ability. On one air combat mission he had disintegrated his opponent and returned with an aircraft damaged by debris and covered with enemy blood; an air battle fought as a real modern tournament.

At the end of November all three squadrons became airborne together for a training formation flight over the Channel. Our past formation practice paid off and I thought we kept station rather well. We landed not too displeased with ourselves, and went to the de-brief half-expecting a verbal commendation from the Wing Commander. Instead of that he pitched in and tore a king-sized strip off us! In his view we had been sloppy, straggled too far and too wide; and altogether would have been easy meat for any German formation we might have encountered. We learned that we needed, and would get, much more practice.

Air Vice-Marshal Trafford Leigh-Mallory, Air Officer Commanding 11 Group, paid us a visit. He had heard about Divoy and me, and we had to tell our story once again. I took the opportunity to plead with him for an attack on the German Kommandantur building in Brussels but in return had to listen to a kindly lecture on the need for overall organisational discipline; and that valuable pilots and machines could not be wasted on hair-brained schemes put up by temperamental young Allied flying officers.

The wing's first operational sortie took place early in December and I was annoyed because I was not detailed for it. Divoy was, and I eagerly awaited his and the others' return to find out 'what it was like over there'. On return, we made it that 603 had lost three pilots and 411 two more. For 64 however, it had been uneventful and most of them did not even know they were under attack. This was one great danger with new and inexperienced squadrons. Concentrating on their formation so much that they allowed themselves to be 'bounced' from the rear.

We acquired a new Commanding Officer. Squadron-Leader Wicks was tall, slim and elegant and quietly but firmly set about the task of teaching us to fly right and he took no excuses for sloppy flying or mistakes. Later 603 went for a well-deserved rest and were replaced by 313, a Czechoslovak squadron.

The news of the Japanese attack on Pearl Harbour was for me personally of less significance than the simultaneous briefing for my first operational flight in Spitfires. The target was an alcohol distilling plant a few miles inland from Dunkirk. Another pilot and I were detailed; but although he had more experience than I they selected me for the leader since I was supposed to be more familiar with the terrain. We needed unbroken cloud cover but half-way across the sea the sky was clear. An abortive return was the only option and I was so upset at this that I earned another little lecture, this time from Wicks, on the virtues of patience, discipline and self-restraint in war.

I did not have long to wait for my next sortie. The following day in fact. It was providing air cover for minesweepers in the Zeebrugge area. Sections of four aircraft from both our own and 411 Squadrons would relieve each other alternatively over the ships. The first two sections of 64 arrived on time and passed an uneventful patrol. 411's section failed to make contact and returned after an hour. Meanwhile a second section of 411 had left for the rendezvous. At their scheduled time of return only one single aircraft joined the circuit. The pilot got down wiping sweat from beneath his helmet. It seems that this section of four had also failed to make contact and, in turning for home, the leader had mistakenly turned over France when he thought he was over the English coast. They had been well and truly clobbered by both Flak and fighters and the other three had all been shot down. Our man had only survived by scraping over and round trees frantically dodging four 109's on his tail. At one time he saw tracer on both sides of his cockpit and had to fly dead straight so as not to veer into the hail of bullets.

When we were not flying missions like these it was practice, practice and still more practice. A fighter pilot is like an athlete, who wins or loses by a split second or a few inches. We had to train hard to gain that vital split-second edge on our opponents.

One afternoon on a cold January day, Conard, another Belgian pilot and I went off for dog-fight practice. For several minutes we twisted and turned all over the sky, with neither being able to get on the other's tail. At one time we found each other hurtling together head-on and I ducked my head in a reflex action as the other Spitfire flashed inches above my cockpit. Two more turns and we were back in the same position closing at a combined speed of six hundred miles per hour. Neither of us wanted to give way. At the last second I kicked hard rudder and slewed to the left . . . while the other pilot did exactly the same but to his right! I felt a slight shock and the airframe of my Spitfire shuddered. I looked out and saw that my right wing tip was missing. Then the other pilot came through on the R/T and he, too, had a wing-tip missing. Everything had happened so quickly we did not have time to be frightened. That came later when we realised what might have been; and when we were stood to attention before Squadron-Leader Wicks who suggested we keep our enthusiasm for the enemy and invited us to 'volunteer' for eight days Orderly Officer duty as well!

Above: 350 Squadron with Spitfire Vs in 1942

Wg Cdr Don ('Kingo') Kingaby, OC Flying at Friston

Flt Off Bentin points a 'Red Indian' badge on Mike Donnet's Spitfire XIV

Escape from
Belgium July 1941. The
Stampe SV4 b with those
who were active in the
escape—above left to right
Mike Donnet—Leon Divoy
—Pierre Valcke and Albert
Valcke—below—Voss, Mark
Donnet, Miche Jansen

Left: **A 'prang' by a pilot of 350 Squadron: Spitfire IVB, AB971**

Below: **NAAFI girl escorted by Belgian officers at Friston, 1944**

Above: **Spitfire XIV of 610 Squadron taken over by pilots from 350**

Right: **Armourer of 350 Squadron at work**

Above: **Gestapo HQ in Copenhagen, March 1945, before the bombing**

Below left: **Mike Donnet's Mustang IV, KM121, after forced-landing**

Below : **The Gestapo HQ ablaze after the attack**

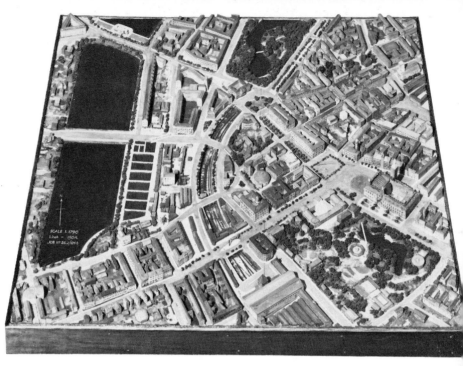

Above: **Relief model made for the attack (at present in the Imperial War Museum)**
Below: **Gestapo HQ after the attack**

Mustang 3D fighters in squadron formation

Mustang 3D of 19 Squadron

Left: **Mustang 3 of 'A' wing photographed by a member of the resistance over Copenhagen showing the attack of the Gestapo HQ**

Mosquito VIs release bombs over the
Gestapo HQ Aarhus (Denmark)
Right: Gliders being towed for the Rhine
Crossing at Wesel, March 1945

The airborne assault across the Rhine
en route to the bridgehead at Wesel
Right: Mosquitos of 2 Group fly over
Copenhagen in August 1945

Above: **Mike Donnet in a Meteor IV, 1949**
Below: **Mike Donnet and Peter Townsend on the day the
French edition was published**

Volunteers were called for to go and shoot-up German barges on the canals between Zeebrugge and Bruges. Conard, Divoy, Flight Lieutenant Taylor and I made up a team of four and once again I was selected as leader because of my local knowledge. Sitting in the cockpit waiting for take-off one felt a little tense but that good healthy bang and growl as the engine started made tension disappear like magic.

We crossed the English coast at thirty feet above sea level so as to be below radar detection height. Unfortunately the suitable weather we had started with deteriorated rapidly. The clouds lowered and visibility fell. Taylor called me on the R/T and asked what I felt about it. I said that I thought it was not too good but I would press-on anyway. Taylor then decided to abort and return to base and it was with a bad grace that I acknowledged his order. Later I realised that he was quite right. A successful operation is where you have all the assets on your side and risks must be carefully calculated. To let eagerness override other factors is fatal. It takes courage to go back in the face of the odds when instinct is wanting to spur you on.

Next day I received a letter from home! I had left Belgium nine months before and since then had been entirely without news of my family. To reach me this letter, sent via Portugal, had taken two-and-a-half months for a trip which had taken me the same time in hours. I felt relieved and happy but shortly after was down in spirits again when I met Conard in the mess and he greeted me with the bald announcement that Offenberg had 'had it'. The most experienced Belgian pilot in Britain and he had to be killed in a stupid flying accident. A trainee pilot making a dummy attack had misjudged his distance and collided in mid-air. His death cast a gloom on all of us. We remembered his escape from Belgium, via a trans-Mediterranean trip in an antique Caudron machine 'borrowed' from the French and with only a compass for navigational aid. We recalled the time when he had been sent off for a gun-test over the English coast but decided to carry it out over the French coast. He had met two 109's "tested" his guns on them, shot them both down and received simultaneously a reprimand and the Distinguished Flying Cross. We would miss him.

It snowed a lot that winter of 1941–1942. Flying was curtailed and the squadron challenged 411 to a snowball battle.

65

They beat us every time, the Canadians having much more snow experience. Some of the Australians and New Zealanders were seeing snow for the first time, and more than one stripped off and rolled in it for sheer excitement.

It was on the morning of one such snowbound and dismal day in February that the CO walked in and for once he showed some sign of excitement as he asked for all available pilots names to be chalked up on the mission board. He said it was a vital operation and the targets would be ships. That was all he could tell us. There were more pilots than aircraft available and we had to toss for it. I lost and watched the others go out to their machines and take-off into a gloomy winter half-daylight. There was a complete blanket of low, heavy cloud, pregnant with snow, overhead.

Later in the morning the news trickled in. Apparently what no one had believed possible had actually happened. The Germans had moved the two pocket-battleships *Scharnhorst* and *Gneisenau* out of Brest and were sailing up Channel, hugging the French coast.

By now the full story of that day is well known. 64's job was to try and keep the Flak defences on the ships occupied so that the Swordfish could go in with torpedoes. The appalling weather made it impossible for them to find any sign or sight of Swordfish or even the ships; and the gallant Swordfish crews went in without any cover. They were all shot down.

Later that afternoon, 64 took-off again and this time I was with them. We flew escort to bombers looking for the ships by now off the Dutch coast. We were in and out of cloud the whole time and mostly more in than out and only occasionally did we even get a glimpse of the bombers we were supposed to protect. One had the feeling that the whole thing was deteriorating into an un-coordinated shambles and perhaps that was not far from the truth. The weather wrecked every plan made that day. The Germans had planned and carried out the escape of these ships in a very efficient way and there is no doubt that the victory was entirely theirs. None of us felt any too happy about events that evening.

There was a little light relief a couple of days later when we were detailed off for 'inter-service liaison' which consisted of me being driven around by a fiery Colonel in a Bren carrier. Unfortunately his driving ability was a little lacking and twice we finished up in a large ditch. I listened to his flow of language with interest and learned many new and interesting English words and phrases!

One Sunday in March 1942 we were in the briefing room again for another bomber escort mission. This time the target was a factory at Comines in northern France. The route lay close to fighter airfields round St. Omer and Abbeville and we thought there might be some action. Intelligence calculated that as many as five hundred fighters could react against us and if they had spent the winter training as hard as us then they would provide some tough opposition.

The entire wing of three squadrons followed each other at low level to the rendezvous point and there we joined up with four other wings. Somewhere in the middle of this buzzing swarm of aircraft belonging to four wings, about a hundred-and-fifty fighters all told, there were twelve twin-engined Bostons who would carry out the actual attack. Over a hundred fighters to protect twelve bombers. The target must have been important! In fact we were out to fight the Luftwaffe.

We climbed to twenty thousand feet to cross-in over France. The Dunkirk Flak batteries opened up on us and we flew through and over rather nasty looking puffs of black smoke. The three sections of 64 were flying in line astern, four aircraft to each section. Everyone was weaving to cover the sky above and behind. Other squadrons were in position stepped up and round the twelve Bostons and the whole vast circus sailed on into France.

Of the opposition there did not seem a sign. Control reported that enemy fighters had taken off from Flessingue and St. Omer but I can only suppose they got lost on the way. We never saw them nor did anyone else. The Bostons reached their target; made unhurried and devastating bomb runs, and formed up for return. We flew back to base and the whole thing was about as exciting as an exercise over England; and just as uneventful.

Divoy and I were briefed the following Sunday for a low-level 'Rhubarb' over the Channel. This meant that we could roam around looking for any likely targets. We were still twenty miles from the coast when the weather suddenly cleared as if by magic and there were blue skies above us. We should have returned, according to the rule, but as I waggled my wings to draw Divoy's attention I saw him grinning at me from his cockpit.

So we flew on. We were so low that our propeller slipstreams were raising foam from wave crests.

A Flak battery at Ostende spotted us and opened up with 40mm stuff. The sea front wall rushed towards me and I thought I saw the battery and aimed the nose of the Spitfire at it at the same time pressing the firing button. I saw rubble flying and a man collapse, then it was past me in a blur. The dunes were already behind and we made a tight turn and swooped down on the airfield of Ostende. There was a hangar and some 109's in front of it. A hangar loomed up before me and I kicked hard rudder to keep my reflector sight on those black crosses on the wings of the 109's. I fired again and suddenly something went crash under my aircraft and I was bursting through thick, grey smoke. I pulled a hard turn to the left. A canal, a railway line and we were out over the sea again and heading for home.

I looked round for Divoy and saw him tucked in on my port side. We could break R/T silence now and he did. His voice came over the earphones.

"Back in time for tea!" He had already realised the important place this fills in English life. It was all worth the rocket we got from our CO for once again breaking the rules.

A few days after this I had my first actual combat. For months now I had wondered what would happen when this moment came. I remembered what Offenberg had told me. "Always watch your tail. If you get bounced, dive straight for the ground and search back into the sun. Whatever you imagine, your first combat is sure to be one thing. It is sure to be completely unlike what you expected."

It was a bomber escort job on Ostende again, and it went straight-forwardly until the bombs were released and the formation was turning for home. Then suddenly the ether came alive with shouts and calls.

"Watch it. Break port!"

"Blue Leader! Where are you?"

"Two, seven o'clock high!"

Control were reporting 'One-fifty plus Calais area' then a few moments later 'A hundred near St. Omer heading towards Ostende.'

I looked out to port and saw a group of about a dozen FW 190's diving down on the bombers. I broke hard left into them and then realised I was by myself. Where was Divoy, my number two ? Suddenly I began to feel very alone. The main formation had gone flying on away from me. I remembered Offenberg's advice and dived for the sea, twisting my neck almost out of joint to see behind and up. There they were. Four black spots closing in on me rapidly. Ours or theirs ? I decided to play safe and assume they were 'theirs'. I did a quick 180-degree turn to face them and recognized FW190's. At the same moment Squadron-Leader Wicks' words came back to me. 'Save that sort of thing for the enemy.' For once I would do exactly as he told me. I went straight towards them firing as I went. I saw red flashes as my shells hit the engine of the leading 190. He passed about three feet over me, so close that he temporarily blocked the daylight out of my cockpit. I just had time to aim a short burst at the second and then I was facing number four. I saw strikes on the FW's wings and cockpit and I was through them.

I did a steep, diving, spiral turn and got down close, very close, to the water. My heart leapt again as I spotted another aircraft coming in from my port quarter then I recognized it as a 411 Spitfire. We joined up, each glad of the other's company and flew back to Hornchurch. Back at base we learned that the wing had lost five pilots. Against that we had one confirmed 'Kill' and five damaged and two of these later were credited to me.

It was a salutary experience. To look back at death closing in apparently without mercy and then to suddenly take the situation by the throat, turn and start fighting to come out the winner. And get away with it. Now I felt a lot more confident but it was a different sort of confidence. Not the over-brash cocksureness of inexperienced youth but the confidence of a man who has been put to a hard test and passed it.

A few days after the events just described, 64 moved again but not very far. Down the Thames Estuary to an airfield at Southend. Our CO, Squadron-Leader Wicks, left us and was replaced by Squadron-Leader Duncan Smith, another ex-Battle of Britain veteran. We gained a new Flight commander in 'Kingo' Kingaby. He was quite a small man but wiry and with quick, adept movements. He had no less than eighteen confirmed 'kills' to his credit and on training flights we soon found out the reason. Twist, dive, turn and spin as we would; in a few minutes the propeller of Kingo's Spitfire would be right on our tail. We were glad he was on our side!

A dawn mission on the 4th April. Fighter sweep over the St. Omer area in an attempt to draw up the Luftwaffe and wear them down with the attrition rate we were sure we could inflict.

It was a glorious morning with blue sky above and fleecy white clouds below. The whole mass of aircraft were in battle formation. It was a big formation and correct station keeping more important than ever. Anyone straying loose in that lot would cause havoc.

Then it happened. I heard someone cry out on the R/T, "Two left high! Coming in fast . . . hold it! They're Spits . . . Christ! What the hell . . . !"

I twisted a glance over my shoulder just in time to see two Spitfires coming straight through the formation. God only knew for what reason. The first flew slap through the middle followed by his number two hanging on close. Even as I opened my mouth to yell a warning I saw the second crash sickeningly into one of ours. It was Divoy's! My hands froze on the stick and I forgot the mission, forgot the formation, forgot everything but that horrible exploding mass of metal as Divoy's machine disintegrated in the air and what was left hurtled sickeningly down and out of sight. With an effort I recovered my sense sufficiently to check my wing tip, separated by only a yard or two from the leader.

I remembered nothing else about that mission. We cruised on but saw no enemy. For me, perhaps, it was just as well since I had no stomach for anything after seeing my old friend, the man with whom I had shared so many dangers; the man indeed who had first started me on the road to freedom; old friend Divoy obliterated in one awful, frightening instant of sudden and violent death. Not in combat but directly through someone else's blind, sinful stupidity!

Back at home I was a little comforted when some of the pilots on the other side of the formation reported that they had seen Divoy bale-out and his parachute open. Someone else had seen the pilot who had caused the crash bale-out near Boulogne.

The next mission, disaster struck again, as if the loss of

Divoy were not bad enough. On another fighter-sweep, Kingo was leading a section of four in the St. Omer area with Conard as his number three and a newly-joined Dutch boy, Jan Plessman, making up the fourth. They spotted two FW 190's flying on a reciprocal heading, passing on the port side. Conard broke hard left after them followed by Plessman, his wing man. Kingaby in front knew nothing of this and his first inkling that something was wrong was when Conard's voice came faintly over the R/T. "One-ninety's behind . . . I see them . . . I see twelve . . . I'm hit!" The leader immediately turned the squadron round calling repeatedly for Conard to give his position but there was only silence and an empty sky.

It was obvious what had happened. The two FW190's had been the bait and Conard, without stopping to think, had taken it. Again and again it was coming home to us that the idea of the dashing, eager fighter pilot rushing all over the sky to get at grips with the enemy was just so much fatal nonsense. Eager, yes, but discipline, discipline all the time in order to stay alive and hit the enemy the greatest number of times. What had they told me earlier? 'We are training you to survive so as to fight and keep on fighting.' A long time after the squadron returned, a lone Spitfire circled the field and landed. It was a white-faced and shaken Plessman. He confirmed what we had already guessed. Before Conard and he realised it, they were in an ambush with at least twelve more FW's all around them. He had seen Conard's aircraft hit and only got away himself by diving to wave-top level. The last he had seen of Conard was of him being attacked by three FW's on his tail.

Five days before there had been three of us from Belgium. Now there was only me. How much longer?

In the next five days I flew five escort missions. Only on two of these did we sight the enemy but he flew high and a long way off, only coming down to bounce anyone unfortunate enough to stray out of the formation on his own.

We now had a newer version of the Spitfire V and I decided to give mine a name as was the custom. I called it 'Old Pyker'. This had been Offenberg's nickname and one of the mechanics did a good job of signwriting for me under the cockpit. Maybe I was a bit superstitious. Perhaps 'Old Pyker' himself might be sitting on the tailplane in spirit form, ready to warn me about enemy aircraft on my tail.

Lunch was cut abruptly short on the next day when we were hurriedly scrambled and deployed to Manston; landing just after 313 Czech squadron whose lunch had similarly been interrupted. On the tarmac we were briefed for a special operation. Intelligence reports said that Goering's train was due in a station south of Dieppe and we were to escort a force of Hurricanes dropping bombs. Half an hour later we were flying at nought feet above the water headed for the station at Neufchatel. Unfortunately an error in navigation brought us in over the French coast at Dieppe instead of Le Treport as planned and we thus lost our course to the target and had to waste time searching and endeavouring to pin-point our position. Obviously the whole operation had become fouled up and the formation leader ordered the Hurricanes to turn back and everyone to use up their ammunition on anything they could find which might be worth it. A lot of locomotives and German barracks really felt our weight that afternoon especially as everyone was feeling frustrated at the abortive sortie and longing to work it off on something.

8

First Blood

On the 30th April, I flew my twentieth operational sortie and it was the third in one day, a total of five hours' 'ops' for the day.

By now the Germans were attacking only on rare occasions and then by making a screaming dive through the formations, firing as they went, and continuing their dive right down to ground level. We were far too many for a depleted Luftwaffe. One could see anything up to ten or twelve squadrons filling the sky . . . between a hundred-and-twenty and a hundred-and-fifty aircraft not counting those ahead or covering the bombers' withdrawal.

Not that we always had it our own way. One day the leader of a section of four from 411 Squadron suddenly realised he was leading not three Spitfires but three Focke-Wulf's; his formation having been shot down behind him. Given a chance the Germans could still be formidable opponents.

A few days later we were briefed for a mission as escort cover to bombers attacking a marshalling yard at Lille. It was a delicate operation which needed precise timing since the supporting force had to arrive over the target at the minute the main force was leaving it. This was the moment when the German fighters would have the tactical advantage being high and up-sun and it was our job to get between them and the bombers turning for home.

As usual we flew low level to the coast then climbed. In close formation we flew towards Lille and could see clouds of smoke where the bombs were hitting their targets.

"Blue 3 . . . Break! . . . Break! . . . Behind you."

Somebody's warning yell brought me alive and I saw Focke-Wulf's screaming down and through us, their leading-edges aflame with gun flashes. I kicked hard rudder and threw the

73

Spitfire round to face them as they dived under me, going hard for the ground. I continued the turn and we sorted ourselves out back into formation. At least by attacking us they had lost their chance at the bombers. I heard someone calling for help. It sounded like a Belgian, Vande-Poel and I also heard another familiar voice, that of his flight commander, de Hemptinne, saying he was on the way.

In five more successive waves the Focke-Wulfs came down on us. Each time we held it until they were almost in firing position then broke hard left to meet them. Try as we would we could not get in behind them for a burst. Using the speed of their high dive they invariably zoomed up high above for another attack.

Walking back to the crew-room at Hornchurch we watched a Spitfire come in over the fence, wallowing and sideslipping as if the pilot could hardly control it. It was Vande-Poel whose appeal for assistance we had heard over the R/T earlier. He had managed to get away from no less than six Focke-Wulfs attacking him . . . and had a hole in his wing large enough to get two men's shoulders through to prove it! Sadly de Hemptinne, whom we had heard going to Vande-Poel's help, failed to return.

That was the pattern of those days. Sometimes one flew several consecutive sorties and never saw a thing. Then would come the next and suddenly it was a desperate fight for survival.

Something like this happened to me in the middle of May. We provided the usual fighter cover for bombers in the Boulogne area. On the ground, spring seemed to be well on the way. A bright sun, hazy horizon and one could clearly pick out the early Spring blossom among the light brown of fresh-ploughed earth strips. I was flying number three to Tommy Thomas while a young American, Jimmy Barrow, was on the other side of Tommy's Spitfire.

"Bandits! Twelve o'clock low. Going down!"

The formation leader's voice crackled over the R/T and simultaneously I saw them. One of our section did not react quickly enough and that, plus Tommy Thomas's sudden dive left a gap . . . with me and Jimmy Barrow in it. I checked over my right shoulder to see if Jimmy was in place guarding my tail and was shaken to see at least fifteen 190's diving on to me.

"Jimmy! Break!"

I pulled hard to the left and went into a spin with engine full on. There was only one thing to do and that was to keep going down flat out, in a steep spiral. My air speed indicator was well over the maximum but even then it felt as if I were crawling ... with half a squadron of 190's behind me! I crossed the coast at nought feet and kicked alternate right and left rudder to see what was happening behind. Four of them were still there. I gave a quick call on the R/T giving my position and the fact that I had company. They closed to six hundred yards and I was just preparing to do a hard turn right about when I noticed them split up; two going on my port quarter and two to the other side. That put paid to my planned manoeuvre. I kept going towards England, turning left and right to spoil their aim. I must have succeeded for eventually they gave it up and broke away back to France. In some Luftwaffe mess that night I was undoubtedly 'the one that got away'.

Kingo Kingaby had also passed an eventful afternoon. He had shot down one FW 190 and then had to fly round and round in circles inside a big cumulo-nimbus cloud whilst the rest of the enemy formation stood guard all round it waiting for him to come out. Finally he had broken out of the bottom, gone hell-for-leather for England—and just made it.

The next day was quite a full day for me. I spent the morning attacking a merchant ship protected by two Flakships outside Calais harbour; and the afternoon in my best uniform explaining to the Duke of Kent about the home-made instrument panel from the Stampe which was on show when HRH opened the new Belgian Club in London. Quite a contrast!

One mission followed another. Once a force of about ten 190's were spotted coming up to us. We were just about to break when we saw more Spitfires coming down at them and within a few seconds four 190's were going down in flames. On another occasion, escorting Hurribombers, we stirred up a hornet's nest of Flak and 190's from nearby Abbeville. The most extraordinary air battle developed with everyone, Germans as well as us, down at nought feet over the water. It was an indescribable mêlée. I must say we felt quite surprised later when the final tally showed we had shot down four 190's with no loss to us. Two Spitfires were badly damaged and got home in a classic case of the blind leading the blind. Johnson, a Norwegian in 64, had a huge Flak hole in one wing and he was leading another Belgian, Wilkin of 122 Squadron, whose instrument panel had been completely shot away.

That day I flew three missions and at the end of it felt completely washed out. In three weeks we had lost two wing-commanders. Peter Powell was badly wounded by a shell splinter in his neck but managed to get back and land at Hawkinge. In his place we got a legend . . . none other than the famous Paddy Finucane. His personal score then was over thirty confirmed; but shortly after he came to us he was hit on a low level mission and ditched. He must have been wounded before hitting the water for he never re-appeared from the wreckage.

It was, perhaps, true that 64 had not been engaged in quite so many missions as others but our score of kills against losses was a better average than most. The fact that our losses were relatively lighter I can only put down to the good discipline which had been drilled into us in the earlier days and which we, as veterans from Turnhouse and Drem, insisted on drilling into newcomers. One example will explain what I mean.

We were flying three sections of four, in line astern with Duncan Smith leading. Suddenly I spotted about fifteen 190's diving from astern. They must have thought they had us cold.

"Ten plus six o'clock, Smitty!" I called.

"Roger." He sounded quite unperturbed. "Wait for my order for a left break." On they came, a thousand yards . . . six hundred yards . . . I began to sweat a little. Four hundred yards . . . this was really tight but not one of us would have budged until Smitty gave the word.

"Break left. Now!"

Like one aircraft the whole twelve of us went into that turn and found ourselves, still in immaculate formation, right behind the enemy. The 190's bent their throttles to get away and although I saw strikes on some of them, that big radial engine of theirs pulled them away from trouble.

It was galling to watch them go but a few days later we were the first squadron to get the new Spitfire IX machines. These had the Merlin 61 giving us 1650 h.p. . . . 400 more than before.

The first time I flew one I wanted to see just what she would do and had an exhilarating fast climb up to 41,000ft. On top of the world! After I landed the CO called me into his office.

"Just what the hell did you think you were doing?" he demanded. I explained that I was just trying out the new mounts.

"And in doing so you have probably given the Germans some valuable information," he went on. "Don't you realise they monitor all our flights on their radar? We're close enough to them. They must know 64 are here. They probably know we have got the new Mark IXs. You've just confirmed it for them. Intelligence is the name of the game, young man."

I left with my tail between my legs but he was quite right, and I cursed myself for not having thought of it. During this period of re-equipment I got permission to bring the little Stampe over to Hornchurch and everyone wanted to look at it. The De Havilland Company at Hatfield also asked me to fly it up there. They were very interested in the Gypsy-major engine which had left their factory before the war and which had now come back in such an unusual fashion.

In July I was presented with the Croix de Guerre at a parade taken by the Minister of Defence. It was moving to be back in a completely Belgian environment once again.

Our first operational sortie with the new Mark IX Spitfire was a very curious affair. We were flying high cover, at 31,000 feet in the Le Touquet area.

"Ten plus eleven o'clock low, Reciprocal heading," called someone.

"One-nineties. And we're up sun and higher. Tally-ruddy-ho!"

Smitty was almost chortling over the R/T.

Then the voice of the ground controller came in our earphones.

"Investigate with caution, Leader. There are Typhoons in your area."

Smitty acknowledged but continued leading us over and into an attack. But that call from ground control had raised a seed of doubt in several minds. Some pilots said later that they had seen what they thought were roundels and held their fire. They could have been excused for this since some German fighters occasionally had circles round their black crosses. Thus the attack went in half-heartedly. Only Kingo did not hesitate and sent a Focke-Wulf, for such they actually were, crashing down into the streets of Boulogne.

Smitty was livid with us when we got back. However, although we had thrown away a chance of doing the enemy a lot of damage when in an ideal tactical position perhaps those who hesitated may have been right. If they had been Typhoons it would have been terrible to have killed Allied pilots by tragic error.

However that same afternoon we had the chance to redeem ourselves. Again we were protecting Hurribombers as high cover and we could clearly see the 190's climbing to attack the Hurricanes. Every time we dived, the enemy formations split up and dodged and we then had to climb back to height again. Still, at least we were keeping them off the Hurricanes which is what we were supposed to do. Once after the climb I saw two 190's below me. I nosed straight down, my number two sticking to me like a leech. I closed in until I was only yards from the tail of one of them, firing steadily with cannon and machine-guns. The 190 seemed to bounce around in the air then, as I broke away hard, I saw him wreathed in thick smoke and falling away. I climbed again and orbited but nothing else came near us.

Thus I had my first confirmed 'kill' and when we totted up we found that 64 had scored five. This was the figure which Smitty had laid down that we would have to get otherwise he would not fly with us again. So we were safe from any further tongue-lashing.

More than that, the action gave us complete confidence in the Mark IX's. Now we felt we were one up on the Focke-Wulf 190's.

At that time the RAF were most anxious to get their hands on a 190 and see what made it tick. The C-in-C Fighter Command itself, Air Marshal Sir Sholto Douglas paid us a visit and commented that so much importance was attached to getting one that perhaps a commando raid might have to be laid on to secure a specimen. Of course it would be necessary for a pilot to go with them, preferably one with local knowledge. He seemed to be looking straight at me when he said it. I wondered if a few names might not already have been put down!

Fortunately an obliging Luftwaffe pilot (Oberleutnant Arnim Faber) saved me from any further anxiety. Attacked by two Spitfires over the channel he shot one down but then, dis-oriented by the whirling combat, landed at Pembrey in South Wales under the impression he was in Brittany. Before he could realise his mistake he was made prisoner and his aircraft captured intact.

We went to Farnborough to have a good look at this adversary we had come to respect. They had flown it there and found that it was fast and manoeuvrable; equal in speed to a Spitfire IX low down but inferior above 23,000 feet. It was very fast indeed in a dive but the Mark IX Spit could outclimb it.

About this time the Germans commenced a regular dusk reconnaissance patrol of two machines, keeping an eye on shipping in harbours around the North Sea and the Channel. In August I was flying an evening patrol looking for them with a Norwegian, Stromme as my number two. We had patrolled up and down for some time with ground control coming through every few minutes with nothing to report for our interest.

"Two bandits confirmed your area," eventually.

"Roger. Searching."

Hardly had I acknowledged when I saw them coming straight towards us. It was almost head-on just beneath a big fleecy cloud and both the Germans and we broke hard to avoid a collision. Stromme and I whirled round and went after them. They began to climb, believing that they would soon lose us but must have been surprised when we 'poured on the coal' and began catching up with them in the climb.

They dived. We followed, dropping our external fuel tanks to give more speed. My eye caught the air speed indicator right round the dial at almost 550 knots! We began that dive a thousand yards away and ended it at six hundred. Stromme called, asking me if I realised where we were. I shot a quick glance over the side and saw the sea on my right. It should have been to the left. This meant we were flying due south and now chasing the two 190's at tree-top height over France. At that moment two more appeared in front, right in my sight. I fired and saw hits registering. Then Stromme came on the R/T again. He was in trouble, with six more on his tail. I turned hard left, saw him dodging and weaving and cut across among his pursuers. They scattered and Stromme joined up with me again.

Fuel was getting pretty low by now. We climbed and called ground control. The controller sounded relieved. We had not been seen or heard of for fifteen minutes and had disappeared suddenly from his radar.

Soon after this we began to fly a different kind of mission. This was as escort to the B17 'Flying Fortresses' of the US 8th Air Force, just getting ready to penetrate into Europe. On our training flights they had seemed to encounter a lot of trouble in keeping formation and were often spread out for miles. On one training flight they were off track by fifty miles and this meant that I ran short of fuel and had to make a precautionary landing on an airfield under construction, fortunately without damaging anything.

I got a few gallons of petrol, enough to fly to Duxford where I landed on my way back to Hornchurch. There one or two of my Belgian friends came to greet me. They were members of 609 Squadron which had been re-equipped with Typhoons. (Amongst those friends was Jean de Selys-Longchamps, an ex-cavalry man who was going to become famous in Belgium in January 1943 when he attacked the Gestapo Headquarters in Brussels. Unfortunately he did not survive the war and met his fate one night in the summer of 1943 on a return from a low-level attack in Belgium.) We discussed in the mess tactics with the Station Commander John Grandy. The Typhoons had been acting as attackers to the Fortresses that day. Had they been Focke-Wulfs, the losses would have been heavy. Thus a change of tactics was vital if the Fortresses were to survive.

The 17th August, 1942 was an historic date when the first of the mighty B-17 formations went into action. They carried no less than 13 heavy-calibre .5in machine guns and a crew of 10 men. Their first target was ground installations near Rouen and the formation was led by Major Tibbett who, three years later, was to drop the first atomic bomb on Hiroshima.

The briefing had called for the overall formation speed to be cut down so that they could remain in more compact formation and be easier for us to protect. We were to rendezvous at 25,000 feet over the English coast, and all three Mark IX equipped Spitfire squadrons would provide the close escort right round the bombers. It was realised that we might have to fight all the way in and all the way out but we felt confident; knowing we now had a good machine with which to tackle the opposition.

The first leg went precisely as planned. There was no opposition, the weather was clear and we could see some impressively accurate bombing of the ground targets. The huge formation wheeled slowly about and set course back for England.

"Bandits! Twenty plus coming in behind the big boys!"

"I see them. Tally-ho!"

This was the Germans' first sight of the 'Forts' and they made the mistake of coming straight in at them without any height or speed advantage. The first two ran into a tremendous concentration of fire from the 'Forts' gunners. Kingo was also firing away like mad at this unfortunate pair. I found myself in a whirling dog-fight with a dozen more milling around my section. Stromme chased one round in circles like a terrier after a rat. I closed with another head-on but at the critical moment my cannon jammed and I only had the four machine guns. Twisting round to face every attack as it came, the fight drifted over the French coast. I saw two below and to the left and was about to dive when caution born out of experience made me look up and see four more sitting up there just waiting for me to go down after the bait. I dived all right, but straight down as hard as I could go for sea level. The Forts had crossed out again heading for England and our job was done. Levelling out over the sea I looked ahead and saw three fighters going my way. I closed on them thinking they were three of ours when I realised it was a lone Spitfire being chased by two 190's. So engrossed were they in closing in for the kill that they committed the fighter pilot's cardinal sin of forgetting to look back. I edged close in behind and got the dot of my reflector sight fairly and squarely on the tail of the rearmost one. I pressed the button and fired a long burst from my machine-guns, the only armament I had left. I saw strikes on his wings. He broke hard left and I had enough time and enough ammunition to get in another burst at the leading one before he too dodged left in a screaming turn.

I came alongside the Spitfire and recognized it as from 403 Squadron. Together we flew back to England, the other pilot giving me a thumbs-up and grinning from his cockpit. Later that evening he telephoned me to say that his aircraft had been damaged and he was incapable of taking evasive action. Had I not suddenly appeared literally out of the blue he would have been a goner. He was very grateful.

The 19th August, 1942. The date of the ill-fated Dieppe raid! Every available fighter squadron in the south of England was briefed to take part in one or other aspect of this operation.

The idea was to maintain air superiority over the beachhead and protect the ground forces. It would not be an easy task since we would be operating over a hundred miles away from base in an area where the Luftwaffe fighter force was deployed in strength.

Somewhat to our disgust, 64 were briefed to fly escort to Fortresses going on to bomb the Abbeville area. We thought we might be missing something! Abbeville was usually a hornets' nest of enemy but as we arrived over it that day we saw nothing in the air. They were all occupied over Dieppe, only thirty miles away. The huge Forts carried out their precision bombing run undisturbed and their attack put the airfield out of action for the day, destroyed many aircraft and killed eight pilots.

One of our pilots, noted for particularly keen eyesight, reported aircraft taking off as the first bombs went down. Over the R/T he requested permission to go down and attack. In return he got a verbal rocket from the Squadron Commander who sharply reminded him that we were there to protect the bombers. Discipline again! They all had to learn.

Back at Hornchurch there was a hectic coming and going with aircraft constantly landing and taking-off and petrol bowsers scurrying all over the airfield. We just had time to land, refuel and smoke a quick cigarette before we were again airborne and this time headed for the beachhead.

Over Dieppe, even from our height as top cover, we could see something of the hell it was down there. Out to sea huge warships were firing from their big guns, wreathing themselves in smoke every time a broadside went off. The occasional batteries were firing back, raising huge waterspouts round the ships. We saw abandoned and burning tanks and vehicles on the beach; and in the streets houses were aflame. In the air individual dogfights developing here and there with black puffs of Flak mixed up with everything.

Over to port I saw a Dornier 217 on fire and trailing smoke with Allied fighters queuing up to get at him. Control warned us of more German fighters at 20,000 feet. We climbed and met them as they were diving. They tried to dive down clear and we followed but other Spitfires lower down got in before us. Duncan Smith went for a Dornier 217 which he left hit and wallowing, and then had to take hard evasive action from another

Spitfire whose pilot should had had nought out of ten for air-craft recognition!

We could only stay thirty minutes over Dieppe and finally had to turn and head home. I landed at Hawkinge and my fuel gauge showed exactly ten gallons when I switched off. All the bowsers were fully occupied so I decided not to wait and took off for Lympne ten miles away. There I got thirty gallons which was enough to get me back to Hornchurch.

Again there was only time to fill tanks before we were off again for Dieppe. The word had come through that things were not going too well on the ground and we had to do our best to keep enemy aircraft away from the troops, fighting amongst the houses and around the docks.

By now the sky was overcast and every pilot, both ours and theirs, was making full use of the cloud. I managed to get an FW 190 dead in my sight at 400 yards but just as I was about to press the button he disappeared into the thick murk. Duncan Smith was bounced by another who popped out of a cloud behind him. He had to bale out but was fortunately picked up later; very much alive and still cursing loudly!

By now the ground forces were pulling out and we held on as long as we could, covering the evacuation. Our final score was three Dorniers and one 190 destroyed and three more enemy damaged. A Polish squadron were claiming eleven kills and 350 Squadron, the first Belgian squadron in the RAF, accounted for nine. That day the RAF lost 113 pilots and claimed 100 enemy shot down.

The Luftwaffe must have had a rough time of it too. The next day there was an enormous sweep of five hundred Allied aircraft over France but they saw nothing.

Fortress escort missions seemed to be our allotted role in the war and we carried them out daily. In one attack we orbited over Rotterdam for twenty-five minutes awaiting the bombers who were late on rendezvous. Fuel began to get low and Ser-geant Dickerson was forced to ditch when still fifteen miles from the English coast. He managed to get into his dinghy and was soon picked up by a fishing boat. For some reason, possibly not expecting to be rescued, he had consumed the whole of the emergency rations in his survival kit and on being put ashore was conveyed to hospital suffering not from ex-posure but indigestion!

I very nearly 'bought-it' myself shortly after this. I was just getting over a heavy influenzal chill and really I suppose I should have done the sensible thing and gone sick. Instead I insisted on carrying out an offensive sweep and was pounced upon by an ME109 eager for a fight. I went through the motions heavy-headed and listless. Somehow none of it seemed to matter any more. It was just too much effort to keep nerves and reflexes tight and alert. Suddenly the sight of his tracer woke me up from this fatal lethargy; I pulled myself together and went into action. I got in a good burst which hit his wing in several places; after which he left me alone.

One very great surprise for us at Hornchurch in September 1942 was when Leon Prevot, CO of 122 Squadron who had been shot down over France at the end of July, re-appeared amongst us and with a remarkable story to tell.

It seemed that he had been hit by Flak over St. Omer and his control column shot away. His Spitfire went out of control and commenced to loop whilst he was struggling to open the hood and bale out. One loop, then a second and each time getting closer to the ground. The aircraft commenced a third loop and at the bottom of this one would certainly hit the deck. At the top Prevot managed to get the hood off and dropped out. There was just height enough for his canopy to deploy before he touched ground. He landed among farm workers in a field. They helped him to hurriedly bundle the 'chute out of sight, to disguise his uniform with mud and earth, then to grab a fork and start hoeing. When the Germans arrived he enthusiastically joined in the search for himself and when the remainder trooped off home he was shouldering his fork in their midst. He was hidden by the Resistance and passed into the 'pipeline'. Three weeks later he was back.

Shortly after this the CO warned me that I was due for a posting to take over a flight in another squadron. I did not like the idea very much because it meant leaving the unit and friends I had been with so long. The CO was very nice about it. "Look here," he said to me. "You've learned a lot. You've learned the tricks of air fighting and how to out-manoeuvre your enemy. More than that, you've learned how to lead and how to control. To control yourself as well as others. Those are valuable abilities, my lad, and they must be made use of."

This made me feel a little better because I knew how many new pilots were joining the squadrons. There were Americans too, eager for advice on air-fighting. Maybe experience passed on in time might help to save some of their lives. The Station Commander, Group-Captain Lott, did make efforts to get me a flight in one of the squadrons of the Hornchurch wing. Group were adamant. I would have to go.

In the event I did not leave 64 but the way this came about made me wish I had. Escorting Fortresses on 2nd September 1942 back from Rouen we met some really strong opposition and Tommy Thomas, 'A' Flight commander, and his number two, George Mason, were both shot down. Later that day they told me that I was to take over 'A' Flight in place of Thomas.

We got a new task entrusted to us. This was to exercise with the P38 twin-boom Lightning fighters of the USAAF then about to start long-range escort missions. The P38's were very fast but not so manoeuvrable as the 190's they would have to face. They lacked rear protection and were limited in diving speed.

On our first mission together we were flying top cover with the P38's as close escort to their countrymen in the Forts. Looking down I saw 190's climbing up to the bombers. The P38's were flying a beautiful formation but completely unaware that the wolves were getting among their flock. We had to dive straight down through them to ward off the 190's from the bombers. They would learn, they would learn!

Late in September we had a mission which became a most awful foul-up. We were one of four Spitfire Mark IX squadrons escorting Forts to Brest. The briefing was a bit hurried and given out on the open tarmac at an airfield near Plymouth. As we walked to our aircraft, Kingaby fell into step beside me. He looked a bit anxious.

"That met. forecast," he said. "It was crazy. I mean, look at it." We both looked up at the clouds racing along before a wind of nearly gale force from the north. The forecast had talked about light southerly winds and this was the wind the bomber navigators would be reckoning on.

We found our bombers above a complete undercast of clouds and escorted them to what we and they estimated was Brest. Then we turned about and, after forty-eight minutes flying, thought we should be over England and that the coast-line we could see through the occasional hole was Cornwall.

Two of the other squadrons went down through this hole. We had no contact with the ground controller and decided to stay at height to try and get a position by radio. Then we heard shouting on the R/T. The two squadrons who had dived down had suddenly found themselves being fired on by Flak and attacked by fighters. We were still over Brittany! As a result five Canadians of 403 Squadron were shot down and a tragic total of eleven American pilots from a USAAF Spitfire IX squadron just formed. The commander of this squadron had been called to London that day and later got back to Biggin Hill to find he had no aircraft and no pilots. In fact no squadron. It was 133 Squadron, the third of the 'Eagle' squadrons and would have transferred next day from the RAF to the USAAF. We were lucky to have stayed at height for there we flew most economically and at a reasonable speed. Even so we reached base with only a few gallons in reserve. In my section our four aircraft could only count ten gallons between us! As if the tragic outcome were not enough the Germans captured a brand new Spitfire IX intact, which they had wanted for a long time.

War had now become a habit. Faces came and went. Stromme went down over St. Omer. In December we flew escort missions from Cornish bases to aircraft en route to the North African landings. We escorted that curious aircraft, the P39 Bell Aircobra, also headed for Gibraltar. It was a miserable Christmas and a cold New Year on this windy airfield on the Cornish cliffs; not improved by the departure of Kingo Kingaby to take over 122 squadron as CO. 64 had a series of new commanders. Duncan Smith went; followed by Tony Gaze. After him Colin Gray and then Bill Crawford-Compton. In the lull after Gray left and before Bill arrived I took the opportunity, being acting CO, to swap my old Spitfire for a brand new one but Bill was an old hand at this game and I did not enjoy ownership of the new one for very long.

Early in January 1943 we went back to Hornchurch, much cheered thereby and in February they gazetted me for the DFC after one hundred sorties. The party which followed was remarkable in that no less than seventeen of us crammed into one London taxi. On arrival at Liverpool Street station the driver could not believe it and insisted on counting us one by one as we got out.

First Blood

On the 15th February, I was escorting Liberators returning from an attack on Dunkirk and was surprised to look down and see one lone FW 190 climbing to attack them. He had eyes only for the bombers and I managed to get down on his tail before he knew I was there. One long burst and he was smoking badly and, turning over on his back, he plunged down to the sea. Pity. He was a brave chap.

9

The Big Day

At the beginning of March, Bill Crawford-Compton was posted and they gave command of 64 Squadron . . . to me! We had quite a party to celebrate. Almost simultaneously the squadron were moved away from Hornchurch to the north of Scotland.

No doubt we were due for a spell of rest from operations but we resented having to go. Arriving in Scotland we found that it seemed to be perpetually cold and wet and as far as the war went, the only way we learned anything about it was from our newspapers. Being, so to speak, away from the action, discipline began to grow a little slack and I had quite a job attending to this and also getting myself, a foreigner, accepted as CO of one of the RAF's famous fighter squadrons with a long and proud history.

We were back on Spitfire V's again and well worn and tired specimens at that. I organised an intensive programme of training including formation flying and night flying. Occasionally we got an escort assignment, usually to the liners *Queen Elizabeth* and *Queen Mary* then serving as troopships and bringing US troops into the Clyde. A night fighter squadron equipped with Beaufighters were based with us. They were mostly New Zealanders and thought, lived and breathed Rugby. We challenged them to a game and were soundly beaten 48 to nil! After that we stuck to soccer.

I had a very mixed bag of pilots of various nationalities. There was Johnny Plagis, a Rhodesian of Greek origin who had shot down twelve in Malta; there were Polish pilots with difficult names and who were liable to do the wildest things unless watched carefully. We even had a West Indian. He was a good pilot but repeatedly got into hot water for doing low-level beat-ups over friends' houses. One Dutchman, Piet Voss, had

88

been an engineer in the Fokker works but escaped from Holland in 1941 in a Fokker G1 fighter, the last of a series being built for the Germans. Altogether twelve different nationalities were represented on 64 Squadron during my term as CO.

We started a new activity when we were required to practise deck landings on a carrier. We tried it out first on the airfield; a specially marked-out area representing the flight deck. Then we made four landings each on *HMS Argus* in the Clyde. All ten of the pilots made their four landings without any trouble ... all except their CO that is, who made a bit of a botch of his first two approaches and only managed it at the third try! I think we were the first squadron to have all its pilots passed out successfully on deck-landings at their first attempt.

We continued to complain about the cold and drizzly Scottish weather. And then one morning we woke up and summer had arrived and the dull, grey countryside had become sparkling with green, rose and yellow and the sky was luminously rain-washed and the air soft and clear.

Then, finally in August we were posted back south. Not to Hornchurch but to Friston, more of a camp than an airfield, on a cliff overlooking the Channel. We did not stay long there and soon moved to Gravesend at the mouth of the Thames. We had a first operation in September, flying escort to Ventura bombers raiding Boulogne. I came in behind a section of four FW 190's and got in a long burst which sent one down to the sea. Plagis and Junior Hardner, a US pilot still in the RAF, also damaged one each.

I was quite pleased with this effort for we were still flying the clapped-out old Spitfire V's we had brought down from Scotland and we had logged more than 4,000 total flying hours on them since the previous April. In addition the squadron's combat discipline had been excellent which showed that the hard training had paid off and that morale was high.

Another move to West Malling in Kent where the station-commander at the time was Peter Townsend, one of the youngest Group-Captains in the Service and a Battle of Britain veteran. Yet a further move followed; up to Coltishall in Norfolk where we settled down for the winter. The sorties we had to carry out from this base led by 'Laddy' Lucas were not unexciting. Every one meant long, low-level flights over the sea. We were flying the Spitfire V, D version, which gave a better speed low down; through modifications to the Merlin engine. However these modifications seemed to be the cause of frequent coolant leaks and an engine failure a hundred miles out from the coast at low-level was not without its problems.

On many of these sorties we were a bit puzzled as to why, whatever the target was, it always seemed to be in open country. Not until later did we learn that these targets were the newly spotted V-1 launching sites; then being prepared in France for the onslaught with these pilotless machines against England.

One day I took a break and flew to Hornchurch to have a look into the ops room. It was fascinating to watch the plaques being slid across the table and to see an air battle actually building up. It seemed like magic to hear the Controller, Ronny Adams, quietly putting Bill Crawford-Compton's wing into a favourable position to attack from a seat on the ground two hundred miles away. Later the aircraft were ordered back to Hornchurch and the plaques removed from the table. I went back to my machine, took-off and was on the ground at Coltishall in time to watch them landing.

In October, we began to escort Beaufighters, armed with torpedoes and rockets, in attacks against coastal shipping in Dutch or German inshore waters. There were usually plenty of Flakships around and the 'Beaus' always got a hot reception.

Coming back from escorting Mitchells in an attack on Schipol airfield I spotted a lone ME 109 just over the coast. I came down hard and fast out of the sun and fired a long burst from both 20-mm cannon and machine guns. He nosed over into a shallow dive smoking heavily. I was credited with a probable.

Finally in November I was posted away from 64 to the Fighter Leaders course at Aston Down. I had been a member of 64 for two years and two months and flown over 300 hours on operations. It was like taking leave of one's family when I finally went.

I was going back to school as an instructor but it was a school for teachers. We had to teach not only the rules of fighter operations but the rules of command in the air as well. We had to teach new tactics of ground support for land forces. We had to practise ground attacks and dive-bombing against vehicles and ground targets.

The Big Day

In February I was back at Hornchurch again but this time for a ceremonial parade to mark the 100th victory by a Belgian pilot. In front of all the Belgian aircrews the Prime Minister awarded the Croix de Guerre to the Air Force Standard. The sight of these three 'colours' which had been given by King Albert the First in 1919 to the famous flyer Willy Coppens, raised some emotion with us. Like us, the colours too had 'escaped', having been smuggled down through France and across the Pyrenees by officers who had escaped in 1940.

The next day I went back to Millfield in Northumberland. There the staff of a new Tactical Air Force which would operate with the invasion forces in Europe were beginning their planning. Later on I was invited to take over a Mustang squadron and I was quite keen to get a chance at this most promising aircraft. I had to clear it with the Belgian authorities but they gave it a definite 'thumbs-down'. Wing-Commander de Soomer, the Belgian liaison officer at Fighter Command headquarters told me that instead of this I would be taking command of 350 Squadron, the first all-Belgian squadron to be formed in the RAF.

So on the 24th March, I stepped out of an Oxford on to the bleak, windswept airfield near Peterhead, north of Aberdeen. The squadron were lined up on parade waiting for me. After that I received a request from the airmen of the unit to be allowed to hold a 'steak-and-chips' party to celebrate my arrival. I asked their spokesman, a tough little Corporal fitter, how they proposed to get hold of steak in rationed Britain. He almost winked at me before confessing that he had found a Belgian-born butcher in the locality who could prepare horse meat in the proper way. I gave permission, the party was held and the steak and chips accompanied by gallons of beer enjoyed by one and all. Not until next morning did several of our non-Belgian guests learn that they had eaten (and enjoyed) horse steak!

Morale was not too good up there in the far north of the country. We were remote from operations and our aircraft were old and worn-out and difficult to fly and service. All the time I was on the 'old-boy' network, pulling strings and trying to get us moved back south with better aircraft. Meanwhile it was the old story of training, training and more training so as to weld the unit into a good, disciplined fighting team.

Whether it was because the authorities finally got fed-up with my badgering I do not know but we got the buzz that a move south was definitely 'on' very soon. Morale promptly shot right up again and late in April 1944 all our twenty-two aircraft set course in perfect formation back to Friston, the south, and the war. Sadly our return was shadowed by a mid-air collision in which Second-Lieutenant Scuvie was killed when he clipped Adjutant De Jaegher's machine shortly after take-off.

We had a new Wing Commander Flying at Friston . . . none other than my old friend Kingaby. I felt it was a good start. On 2nd May, we took part in our first operation; escort for Marauders attacking the marshalling yards at Valenciennes. Our wing was composed of ourselves, 345, a Free French Squadron and 501, one of the famous English Royal Auxiliary Air Force squadrons of pre-war days.

Maybe some of the younger pilots thought it exciting enough but for me it was all very strange. Strange because all we could see in the sky were Allied aircraft. Where was the Luftwaffe? Maybe they had all been moved to the East front for if they had been here I am sure they would have come up and had a go at us. A year ago there was an FW 190 lurking behind every cloud but now all the airfields we flew over were deserted; or appeared so. In vain did some of our aircraft beat-up their runways to try and lure them into the air. There was just nothing doing.

Coming back over England we could clearly see the harbours beginning to crowd up with shipping; and long queues of men, vehicles and equipment on the roads. It was obvious the invasion would come soon.

On the 4th June, Kingo was called to 11 Group headquarters and came back smiling. He took me on one side and quietly whispered to me that this was it. Tomorrow was the big day— or the day after, if the weather were to turn out bad on the 5th.

In late afternoon pilots were called to the briefing room and all personnel were confined to camp. In the briefing room Kingo told us about the invasion plans. Everything, that is, but where it would actually take place. We had maps of France on the walls and everyone had his own pet theory and claimed to know just where it would be. There was electricity in the air. This was it! This was what many of those in the room had undergone privation, hardship and passed through many acute dangers for. The next day they would start on the job of freeing their countries and their loved ones from the invader. Even the mechanics working around the aircraft outside had caught an inkling of what was happening and several times looked out to sea as they worked with an eager emotion.

Then the word came through giving the spot selected for the landings. Already aircraft were on their way carrying bombs, towing gliders filled with paratroops. The whole intricate machine of war was on the move. As one of almost one hundred and seventy-five Allied fighter squadrons, our job would be to give continuous air cover over the beachhead day and night.

On the morning of the 6th June, 1944 Captain de Patoul, the adjutant, wrote in the squadron diary:— "978th day of 350 Squadron's existence. After a period of adolescence, full of enthusiasm and team spirit, it now enters a new phase, that of maturity armed with its experience and its reputation. It is ready to honour the past and look to the future with confidence. 19 enemy aircraft destroyed; 22 damaged. It is not the end; it is the beginning of the end!"

Our mission for this 'longest day' were three squadron patrols to protect the initial landings and give fighter cover to the amphibious forces and over the beaches. We would have to operate before dawn until well after dusk and we needed our night-flying training on which we had concentrated for the last three months. This had been a lesson from experience. Lack of continuity of air cover at the period between daylight and dark had been a serious problem in the Sicily and Italian landings.

We were awake at 4.30 a.m. and took off, twelve strong, whilst it was still dark. Thus we had grandstand seats to watch the mighty drama being enacted below. We saw the capital ships throwing their huge shells against the beach defences from eight miles out to sea. We watched the approach of the first assault craft, their long, parallel wakes like ploughed furrows in the water as they headed for the beaches. We could count the gliders lying lop-sidedly in the patchwork fields. The only thing we did not see was an enemy aircraft.

Back at base the pilots were surrounded by eager ground-crew wanting to know how it was going. They wanted to know every detail of this vast operation; an operation which was going to get them back home amid friends and family. We told them what we could.

Back on patrol again mid-morning, and again 'nothing to report!' The last patrol of the day was from 2200 to 2400 hours and this time it looked more of an inferno than ever down below with huge gun flashes out to sea; explosions and flames along the coast and tracer scudding across as the Allies fought their way inland.

Next day we spotted two German fighters but they were away out of our reach before we could react. On the next patrol low cloud forced us down and we had to dodge Flak from both sides, theirs and ours!

We scoured the area at low level but again no sign of the enemy. Even so we were not without losses. Bertje Herreman was killed when his Spitfire collided in cloud with a Marauder. Then Alexandre's engine failed on the way out and he was drowned, ditching in a choppy sea. When his wingman returned I had a row on the telephone with Paddy Crisham the Sector Commander who would not let me take-off and search for my flight commander. He finally gave way. I ran to my aircraft and was able to guide the air/sea rescue launch into the reported position but they searched in vain.

Thus it continued, three missions a day throughout those first days when the troops were fighting for a hold. Roberto Muls, one of my pilots, had an engine failure over the beach and forced-landed on it. Thus he was the first of our bunch to set foot on the newly-liberated continent of Europe! On his return we gave him a symbolic yellow jacket; as is the custom with the daily leader in the famous Tour de France bicycle race.

Morale was slipping again because we were flying long hours and had nothing to show for it; and in worn-out old aircraft at that. We had a visit from M. Gutt, the Belgian Defence Minister, and he had to listen to a load of complaints from us. Anyhow at the beginning of July we were hurriedly whisked from Friston to Westhampnett near Chichester, where we found eighteen Mark IX Spitfires, including three brand-new ones, waiting for us.

They seemed destined to be wasted for still there was no sign of the Luftwaffe. Then we had a briefing for an exciting operation. No less than an attack on the German Kommandantur in Brussels. However for some reason this operation was cancelled.

On the 24th July, we were flying close escort to aircraft bombing the Falaise Gap, rapidly narrowing with the German armies trapped in the pocket. 349 were low cover and we were on top. Suddenly the Luftwaffe appeared in the shape of about a dozen ME 109's which came out of the sun, down on to the bombers. 349 got itself engaged in sorting them out whilst we put ourselves in a good position for an attack.

"One bandit eleven o'clock. Low heading south."

Even as Jean Lavigne, my wingman, called I saw the lone 109 With Jean hanging on behind I dived flat out behind him . . . 500 yards . . . 400 yards . . . my finger was about to press the button when something made me pause. There seemed a rather odd shape about this 109. I overhauled and discovered it was a Spitfire from 349 Squadron flown by Paul Siroux, one of their flight commanders. And I had nearly shot him down!

The prospect of once again getting back to a freed Belgium was looming larger and larger and those last few days of 'sweating it out' were intolerable.

A few mornings later some of us were awakened by a curious throbbing noise; like an aircraft engine but unlike any we could put a name too. Suddenly it stopped and a few seconds later, even those still sleeping were roused by an almighty explosion nearby. Thus the first of the new pilotless 'secret weapons', the V-1, had arrived.

From then on they became a regular part of our day, and one listened with close attention to that pop-pop-pop noise of the ram-jet engine; hoping it would go on popping for once it cut out then you knew that the thing had gone into its dive to explode when it hit the ground.

We were one of the squadrons detailed off to attack these fiendish things. At first it was rather a shambles because the appearance of one in the air was a signal for any fighter within sight of it to join in the attack and generally end up getting in each other's way. However, this situation was quickly sorted out and a system evolved whereby the fast Mustang III aircraft were at them first out to sea; backed up by a tremendous force of anti-aircraft guns rapidly deployed along the coast, and behind the guns another force of Tempest, Spitfire XIV and the new, still secret, Meteor 1 jet-fighters. Our particular zone of operation was between the coastal guns and the London balloon barrage and we patrolled a 'lane' about 50 miles wide. Even this was something of a narrow constraint for a Spitfire XIV flying at 400 miles an hour low down. The re-equipment with these brand new Marks of Spitfire had come consequent upon our move to Hawkinge on the cliffs near Dover from where we could actually see the French coast in clear weather.

The V1's were flying over night and day and we had several 'incidents'. One came down near the dispersals and three Spitfires were blown into fragments. Another day the ceilings in the requisitioned house we used as a Mess collapsed when one hit close by. These new weapons we did not like. We could face any human enemy but these new soulless, mechanical menaces; nasty and anonymous which arrived like a comet leaving a long, red glaring tail behind them were different. Hawkinge was right in the middle of 'Flying-Bomb Alley' and at one time there were about two hundred aimed every day!

We had sufficient speed to catch them and one of our pilots on one occasion, having exhausted his ammunition without destroying the thing, flew alongside and, carefully judging his distance, managed to tip its wing, upset its gyroscopic control device, and saw it make a curving dive to earth. After that tipping them off course became a recognized attack technique and many were destroyed this way.

New gun-laying radars firing shells fitted with the 'variable time' proximity fuse eventually became so efficient that as many as 90% of all V1's were shot down over the coast. The Allied advances in France and capture of the launching sites saw the menace eventually die away. Not before time.

The war in Europe had now turned into one of vast troop movements on the ground. Flying units which had at first been deployed to Normandy now found that the forward Allied troops were beyond their radius of action and were returned to bases in England. We too, were frequently called upon for ground support which meant low level attacks against trains, vehicles and any form of enemy transport we could find.

It was on 3rd September, 1944 that, on landing from just such a sortie in the Louvain–Brussels area (echoes of four years earlier!) the squadron adjutant came running out to my aircraft almost with tears streaming down his face. They were tears all right, but tears of joy for the news had just come through. Belgium had been liberated!

Never was the 'Brabançonne' listened to with more emotion

than at lunchtime next day in the Mess. Four years of fighting, hardship, death and tragedy and now the reward. I saw men on the squadron whom I had always thought tough, cynical characters unashamedly weeping. Friends from the RAF, and from Canadian, Australian, French and Dutch units all came and shook our hands delightedly with as much joy as if it had been their own country.

Next day an offensive sweep was planned and I asked for, and received, permission to fly over Brussels on the way back. I selected twelve pilots all of whom had homes in the capital. Over the city we flew low in a wide V formation along the main boulevards. As I came over the Porte de Namur I banked steeply and hurled a large Belgian flag from the cockpit addressed to M. Van de Meulebrook the Town Mayor, and which all my pilots had signed. I saw it unfurl in the slipstream and float down, its black, gold and red flapping over the City. What a pity that it never reached its intended destination. Some heartless souvenir-hunter purloined it en route.

On the 8th September, four of us got permission to go back to Belgium for a few hours. I landed at Evere, scene of so many memories of my early days. What a lot had happened since I was last there. None of us had talked much on the way across. We were all a little too full of private feelings. For myself I was seeing in my mind's eye many faces. Faces of those who would never see a free and liberated Belgium again.

From Evere I took a tram. The same sort of tram I used to take in the old days. A bit worn and battered after several years' war service but who cared so long as it kept going. And keep going it did, right up to the corner of my street, I walked up and pushed open the gate. The squeak was still there!

No need to try and describe my next hour. It was a confused babble of welcome and joy.

The city was in a feverish state of excitement. There were people and uniforms everywhere and on every side sheer unbounded happiness and joy. I got back to Evere and found my three pilots waiting. This was what three years of discipline had done for us. At one time we would have scrounged more time but an hour later we were back at Hawkinge reporting to a very surprised Group-Captain Maxwell who, despite his condition that we were to return the same evening, was convinced he would have four pilots 'adrift' for a few hours longer (but who was prepared to be understandingly lenient if they were!)

That evening in the mess we had a party and there were many old friends present. These included Miche Jansen who had done so much to help Divoy and I escape. He had quite a story. In 1942 he had been arrested by the Germans as a prominent Resistance man, and sentenced to death. In prison at St. Gilles, waiting for the sentence to be carried out, he had escaped and got to England. Nothing would satisfy him but to get on operations in the air but they told him he was too old to be a pilot. So he became a tail gunner on Mitchell bombers. Some time before we heard with great joy that Divoy was still alive. Apparently after bailing out of his tailless Spitfire after the collision, he had been temporarily blinded by engine oil and could not see the ground. His landing by parachute was consequently very awkward and he broke a leg. He had been taken prisoner and was at the moment in the notorious Stalag luft III impatiently awaiting the end of the war. Jansen and I drank a toast or two to him.

The V1's had gone but the V2's had arrived. These neither we nor anyone else could do anything about. The first you knew one was imminent was when it exploded on landing from outer space.

We carried on giving the ground forces support and cover over Holland and Germany. We escorted the tugs and gliders and the re-supply Dakotas to the Arnhem operation and regretted bitterly the failure to link up the battling Airborne troops with the main Army front bogged down just a few miles to the west.

Then we moved to join 83 Tactical Group on the mainland of Europe. We moved all right, but only to Lympne a few miles away. What is more, to add insult to injury they took away our new Spitfire XIV's and left us with 130 Squadron's worn-out machines. I made the 'phone wires red-hot with complaints to the Belgian Authorities and eventually wrung from them a promise of a certain move to Belgium before long; and that something would be done about our Spitfires. Then they got their own back on me by telling me that although the Squadron might go, I wouldn't! Instead I was posted to Hawkinge as Wing-Commander Flying for the RAF Wing there. I was happy about the promotion but sorry to leave my Belgian friends.

I returned to the Spitfire IX and to leading a wing made up of 132 and 441 Squadrons, both recently back from France. Again we found ouselves flying bomber-escort and I had much to do reminding pilots who had been so long on free-roaming ground attack missions about the rules of air fighting. One of our first missions was escorting the Dakota which carried Sir Winston Churchill to Paris. I enjoyed having a good look at Paris from the air without having to bother about dodging anti-aircraft defences.

I heard news of 350 Squadron from time to time and not all of it good. Morel had been killed when he stalled on landing. Whether he had some premonition or not we shall never know but it is a fact that when his belongings were being checked they found a sealed envelope to be opened by the officer doing the checking. Inside was a five-pound note with which was the accompanying note "You may all drink my health".

It was a cold winter. Some of our escort missions were as long as three hours in the air, at high level and with no heating in the aircraft. After some of these we needed almost as long to thaw out! 132 were replaced by 450, an Australian squadron fresh from sunny Italy. They just did not believe our warnings about the cold around the European skies and on their first mission took off in their normal Southern European flying kit. On landing we had to carry most of them from their cockpits, they were so stiff with cold. It took hot baths and several whiskies to restore some semblance of life. After that they went to the stores as one man and drew all the warm gear they could lay hands on.

The New Year came and, in February 1945, I was posted to Bentwaters in Suffolk to take over command of a wing made up of three RAF Mustang squadrons. I noted with pleasure that one of them was 64, my old unit with whom I had first gone to war from England. Fine aircraft though the Mustang was, I felt sorry at parting after so long with my old love, the Spitfire.

My first mission as wing-leader was an RAF bomber escort task to Wesel, the Rhine crossing point. I found the Mustang 3 C a comfortable aircraft to fly and at altitude gave the impression of slipping easily through the air. Two days later we were part of a vast effort of offensive missions which had the aim of systematically paralysing the road and rail transport system in North Germany. In all about 5,000 aircraft took part, including some from North African bases.

Next day we escorted 16 Lancasters, each specially modified to carry 20,000 lb. bombs, in an attack on the rail viaduct at Paderborn. On this and all the other missions we met no opposition. It was the last days for the Luftwaffe and although one or two made occasional brave attacks on these vast armadas there was nothing which could be called a real defensive effort. Day after day it was round-the-clock bombing of German transport and communications systems. I led my wing escorting precisely 1,065 Halifax and Lancaster bombers attacking Essen. The next day, 1150 bombers hit Dortmund. It meant a stream 100 miles long and 200 yards wide! A far cry from 1941 when five or six hundred fighters were used to escort six or twelve medium bombers. And they were needed!

10

The Last Attack

On the 21st March, we had a sudden move to Fersfield near Norwich and a briefing for a very special operation planned for the next day. Mustangs from 64 and 126 squadrons were involved with a force of Mosquitoes from 140 Wing. The mission was to be on Copenhagen and I must say that the thought of a long over-water flight followed by a crossing of the Danish islands and mainland had me a little anxious. It was 200 miles over the sea and 250 miles over enemy-occupied territory and all the way back. Whatever Luftwaffe forces were there were capable of a concerted defence, they were all in Schleswig-Holstein and ideally placed to cut us off.

In the briefing room they had set up a wonderful scale-model of the city and the target set everyone off in a buzz of excited talk. None other than the Gestapo Headquarters building! It was to be a similar attack to the ones already carried out on Gestapo headquarters at The Hague; and Aarhus, also in Denmark. These two precision attacks had got the Germans worried about the Copenhagen headquarters so in anticipation of just such an operation as we were now planning, they had put cells on the sixth floor of the building and held prominent Danish resistance and political leaders in them as a sort of insurance for their own precious skins. Thus not only had one building and one building alone in the middle of a large city to be singled out but also the ground floors had to be attacked without damaging the upper ones! It was being carried out at the request of the Danish Resistance whose whole organisation was in danger of collapse from Gestapo penetration.

The Mosquitoes were to carry out the actual attack and 64 and 126 squadrons were chosen for the escort because of their long-range ability. Not only were we to fly escort but we were also to attack Flak positions near the target in order to help the Mosquitoes with their highly-accurate precision run-in.

We were briefed by Air Marshal Basil Embry, AOC 2 Group, who outlined the precautions we would have to take so as to ensure a minimum of civilian casualties. Eleven-second delay-fused bombs would be used to give Danes held in the building a chance to escape.

Group Captain Bateson would lead the Mosquitoes and he gave us the flight-plan. Low-level across the North Sea in strict radio silence. We would be in one whole formation with three separate Mosquito flights of six, followed by two 'Mossies' equipped with cameras. At the island of Seeland, Bateson would broadcast the code-word "Umleitung" (German for 'diversion') once, and we would then split up; the first six aircraft going on ahead, the rest completing an orbit of lake Tisso to achieve separation. The second six would then break off whilst the remainder made another orbit. Over Rosklide we would pick up the road and railway for Copenhagen and over Fredricksburg turn fifteen degrees left for the run-in to the target.

I decided to put twelve Mustangs with the first lot of Mosquitoes while the second and third Mosquito formations would have eight as escort, four each side. Before the briefing was over Storrar, of 234 Squadron, arrived with an extra four Mustangs, intended as back-up, spare machines. Since they were there we decided to include them and their job was worked out as an attack on the airfield at Vaerlose north of the city just in case any enemy fighters were based there and might be taking-off.

We had navigation briefings, memorising landmarks and turning points very carefully; and studying the city model from all angles.

The last part of the briefing was really interesting. It was given by a Major Truelsen of the Danish Army. In 1944 he escaped from Denmark just as the Gestapo were closing in on him. He had been one of the most active and important members of the Resistance and special efforts were made to get him out of the clutches of the Gestapo. Through his connections in Denmark he had much vital information to give us about the exact location of anti-aircraft units and he had helped in planning the route so as to take it clear of strongly defended areas.

Major Truelsen was able to point out many details of the

Gestapo headquarters located in the Shell building in the centre of the city. Through his contacts he repeated that the whole raid was at the strong insistence of the Danish Resistance. Many of their leading members had been caught and jailed in the Shell building and he pointed out that even a day of delay might mean that some of them would be executed before the chance of escape was offered by a successful air attack. That such an attack would have to be carried out with really pin-point precision and timing went without saying. Planting a bomb in an exact spot with a tolerance of only a few feet at almost 400 miles-an-hour was not going to be easy.

I gave my part of the briefing, detailing 126 Squadron in the lead, 64 to escort second and third Mosquito formations; and 234 to cover the withdrawal.

Scheduled time over the target was to be precisely 1115 hours and take-off was at 0840. Thus we would hit the place in mid-morning when the majority of the Gestapo officials could be expected to be in their offices.

The formation took off at timed intervals and formed up over the airfield. Visibility was good as we headed out to sea and set course east, but there was a strong wind which gave everyone a bumpy ride. The waves just below us were very choppy and anyone's chances of a successful ditching in them would not be good. We hoped it wouldn't be necessary.

Just before reaching the Danish coast the bomber navigation leader altered course slightly. Using binoculars he had picked out his landfall mark, a lighthouse, whilst we were still well out to sea, and in time to check for any undetected drift there might have been. We crossed the flat fields of Jutland in one roaring formation, stirring up flocks of birds. One of 126's Mustangs suffered a bird strike and the pilot broke radio silence to tell us.

"Return blue three. Also escort."

It was all the radio talk I could permit myself. I hoped they had both literally 'got the message'.

Farmers working in the fields looked up in alarm, then waved their spades and forks as they recognised our roundels. The aircraft flying number two to the lead Mosquito was sticking close in a very tight formation. I chuckled as I watched. The pilot of this machine was down in the records as 'Wing-Commander Smith' but I and the whole formation knew it was really the Air-Officer-Commanding himself, Sir Basil Embry, turning a Nelson eye to a regulation which forbade him to fly over enemy territory.

We saw the island of Funen looming up ahead in the grey, misty waters and beyond it the lake which was the point where the formation would start to disperse. "Umleitung!" Just one word from the leader's aircraft. The second formation immediately went into an orbit to starboard. The first Mosquitoes bored steadily on, flanked by their Mustang escort. One complete circuit of the lake and the second batch straightened up on a heading to the city. One more orbit and the last six were on their way.

"Target in sight!" This was the lead aircraft calling.

Still the Gestapo officials in the building were blissfully unaware of the devastation even then roaring down on them from the sky. One of the prisoners, Captain Borking, said later that at that moment, having been called for interrogation, he was standing between two armed sentries facing his tormentors. Through the window he saw an aircraft diving down and immediately recognised it as, if not British, then not German. Acting on impulse he put his hands under the heavy wooden table in front of him and flung it over against the two sentries. At that moment the first bomb fell and, with the sentries reeling and bewildered, he ran into the corridor.

The first five Mosquitoes let their bombs go in quick succession, then raced flat out at ground level. The Mustangs meanwhile were strafing the gun positions but so effective had the surprise been that these were not even manned and the guns still had tarpaulins over them.

Wing-Commander Kleboe, leading the second formation, failed to spot a signal mast on his bombing run-in and hit it with one wing. Before he could try for a forced landing the wing broke off in the air and his aircraft plunged into the ground and exploded.

The first group of aircraft had cleared Copenhagen and were turning on course for home when their delayed-fuse bombs went up. All was noise, smoke, flames and confusion on the ground floors of the building. This became worse when the second wave struck. At this time the third formation were just starting their run-in. By now the Flak crews from the German warships in the harbour had taken their positions and more guns began to open up. One Mustang of 64 was hit by Flak and crashed in the middle of the town.

The second formation fared worse than the other two. Puzzled by the flames from Kleboe's Mosquito burning on the ground as well as the flames from the building some distance away, Wing-Commander Iredale ordered his six Mosquitoes to make an orbit whilst he sorted things out. Then he straightened up and both he and his numbers two and three dropped their bombs right into the building. Two others, however, aimed by mistake at the burning Mosquito and their bombs fell very close, but too close to a nearby Convent where over a hundred children were at school. The building immediately started burning. Sadly and tragically, eighty seven of these children and twenty-eight adults were killed.

Meanwhile, in the Gestapo building itself, those of the prisoners who escaped had dramatic stories to tell. Lijst Hansen, a police officer held under suspicion, had been told only that morning that he was being sent to a concentration camp. There had been a delay because of a mix-up over transport and his guards had put him back in his cell on the sixth floor. Thus he was there when the first bombs fell. Realising quickly what might be happening he attacked the cell door with a heavy oak stool and finally, choked with rubble-dust and smoke, battered a hole big enough to crawl through. Then he stopped in amazement for where there had been a solid corridor wall there was now nothing but open space and a magnificent view of Copenhagen from six floors up. Hansen turned and saw the German corridor guard standing staring at where the wall had been, obviously still in a dazed state. Hansen broke into a run towards him yelling for the keys as loud as he could. The guard automatically handed over the bunch without a murmur. Hansen got busy opening cell doors all down the corridor. In ones and twos the prisoners swarmed out and ran for the stairs. Professor Brandt Rehberg and Morgen Fog were among them and at the bottom of the stairs stopped aghast at the sight of several bodies of Germans killed in the attack lying among the rubble. Both paused, blinking in the sunlight, half-expecting to hear shouts and shots behind them then, as they realised that all the Gestapo personnel who had not been killed in the first attack were in shelters, they ran for the open street. A tram was just pulling away from a stop and they leaped aboard . . . just as Captain Borking, covered in dust and plaster, heaved himself up on the platform from the other end. Two brothers, named Alnfeldt-Molletrup had been held in the building. One was killed but the other joined the scramble down the stairs and across the courtyard. He went straight into a barber's shop next door, and after a while, when the Germans had recovered and began scouring the district, he was covered in lather in the barber's chair and quite unrecognisable.

Most of the other prisoners who had escaped were taken care of by the Danish Resistance people who had been watching events from carefully chosen observation points all round the building. Numbers of them were smuggled across to Sweden over the next few days.

In the final count, 27 prisoners escaped out of the 35 'liberated' in this unusual fashion. About 150 Germans were later reported as having been killed. The attacking force lost four Mosquitoes and two Mustangs but one of the Mustang pilots was saved. Apart from the tragic error which led to so many children being killed the raid was a 100% success and was a magnificent example of precision bombing; having as its objective not only destruction of the enemy occupied building but also the avoidance of damage to buildings in close proximity.

This operation was a fine example of a joint all-out effort made by the Resistance members in occupied countries and the Royal Air Force to win the struggle and regain freedom.

The day after this exciting sortie we were escorting heavily laden Dakotas packed with troops, in the Allied crossing of the Rhine at Wesel. At first the German Flak guns claimed victims among the transport aircraft but after fifteen minutes intensive working-over by rocket-firing Typhoons the Flak was silenced.

So accustomed had we become to seeing and meeting no opposition that we were badly caught out over Hamburg a week later when no less than twelve Messerschmidt 262's came down out of the sun on the formation we were supposed to be protecting. By the time we had dropped our cumbersome wing tanks and opened throttles, eleven bombers had been shot down. We accounted for four 262's.

I got behind one 262 and had him right in the sight at 300 yards . . . then my engine died on me! I started to glide down but at 10,000 feet the motor picked up again as suddenly as it had stopped. Luck was still on my side as was evident when an escort for bombers over Kiel was laid on. I had taken a forty-eight hour pass but was strongly tempted to cancel it and go on this mission. Maybe I am superstitious but I thought it was tempting fate to fly on operations when you had planned to be on leave. In fact lots of the chaps had a 'thing' about this. As it happens I had an engine failure on the approach to Dunsfold airfield and had to make an emergency landing. Had I been on a mission I would have had this same aircraft and suffered this same engine failure . . . but over the cold North Sea between Jutland and England . . . not an ideal place in which to get picked up.

On the 6th May, 1945, I flew my last wartime sortie. This was escorting Beaufighters on low-level anti-shipping strikes between Denmark and Sweden. We were out looking for German Navy units who, despite an imminent surrender, were thought to be heading for a last stand in Norway.

The 'Beaus' had a glorious time, attacking odd destroyers and once a pack of four U-Boats on the surface. One destroyer blew up and the U-Boats made hectic crash-dives for safety. Later, we met three other submarines this time escorted by a sizeable Flakship bristling with guns. Both 64, my old squadron, and 126 were on this operation and the latter were commanded by Arne Austeen, an old Norwegian friend, who had been with me on 64. I saw his three sections move over to echelon port and he called to me on the R/T that he was going down after the Flakship. His squadron nosed over and were met by a hail of fire from the ship. Arne received a direct hit and his aircraft exploded and fell into the sea, a mass of blazing wreckage. All those years of airfighting and a few hours before the end of the war, one of my oldest friends, killed in seconds.

We had been in the air over five hours and landed at the airfield at Luneberg in north Germany. Operations warned us to stand-by for another operation next day and so we made it an early night.

About eleven o'clock that night, just as we were all sound asleep someone came whooping and shouting through the rooms making sure everyone was awake. Others came running to say that the Germans had signed an armistice, effective from eight the next morning and so there would be no 'ops' next day, nor the day after, nor ever at all in the foreseeable future.

A great deal of whisky was drunk that evening and a great

deal of pent-up stress and emotion released. Next day when we got back to Bentwaters, the place seemed strangely quiet. It was the first day in years without an almost continual buzz of aircraft noise overhead throughout the day, and half the night.

On the 8th May, we all paraded in front of the control tower and heard the old warrior, Winston Churchill, announce the end of the war in Europe. After that I stayed at Bentwaters. There was still a war in the Far East and youngsters to be trained. I was still there in August when Japan surrendered.

This time peace was really with us. At last the time came for me to say good-bye to my friends in Bentwaters. As I drove to the station I looked at the vast, upturned bowl of sky over the quiet Suffolk fields and every cloud drifting across was the face of someone I had known and who had not returned. What were their names? I could not remember. All I could remember were some lines from a French poet. Let's see, now. How did it go . . . ?

> "And on stones, blood, paper or ash
> I write your name,
> "On the fields of the horizon, on the wings of birds,
> I write your name,
> "On the steps of death,
> I write your name,
> "I was born to know you,
> To name you . . . Freedom."